CAREERS WORKING WITH

ANIMALS

First published in 1981, author Helen Young
New editions 1983, 1986
New editions 1988, 1990 by Helen Young and Vivien Donald
Sixth edition 1992 by Vivien Donald
Seventh edition 1996 by Vivien Donald and Allan Shepherd
Eighth edition 1997 by Allan Shepherd
Ninth edition 2001 by Allan Shepherd

Kogan Page Limited
120 Pentonville Road
London N1 9JN

British Library Cataloguing in Publication Data

A CIP record for this book is available from the British Library.

ISBN 0 7494 3644 1

CAREERS WORKING WITH

ANIMALS

ninth edition

Allan Shepherd

KOGAN
PAGE

Contents

Introduction

Is this the Job for You?

☐ Is it important to you to spend most of your working life with animals?

☐ Have you spent any length of time caring for an animal?

☐ Are you prepared to spend time learning skills and training for a qualification?

☐ If you have to, are you prepared to accept low wages as a price worth paying for job satisfaction?

☐ Are you hard working?

☐ Are you physically fit?

☐ Do you want to work outdoors?

☐ What sort of relationship would you like to form with the animals you work with?

☐ Are you prepared to put the animals in your care first, before any of your own considerations?

☐ Can you cope with the demands animals make without losing your temper or inflicting cruelty on the animals you work with?

Our relationship with animals is a complex one. We easily distinguish between those we keep as pets, those we use as working animals, those we race, those we eat, those which help us to protect or enhance our lives and those which we protect in their natural habitat. Then there are those animals that others have neglected, bullied and abused, and that need a special kind of care.

This book reflects the eclectic nature of this broad employment area and provides information on a wide range of careers, from agriculture to zoos. For each job mentioned there is a description of the type of training you need, the sort of work you will be doing, the opportunity for advancement and the level of wage you might expect when starting out.

Also listed are the various organisations that help individuals to fulfil their aspirations by offering in-depth advice on careers and courses. If this book is the first step towards finding a career working with animals, then these organisations will help you to move on to the next stage, be it finding work experience, choosing a course, starting a modern apprenticeship or in some cases getting your first paid job.

Each chapter contains a number of case studies. This is your opportunity to find out what the people who already work with animals have to say about their jobs, their lives and their aspirations. These case studies can help you decide whether or not a job seems right for you. Take this example: 'Looking after a herd means getting up about 4 am and you can't just go back to bed if it's raining or you had a heavy night the night before.' You'll know straight away whether this is you or not.

With such a wide range of careers to choose from, how will you decide which one is right for you? Sometimes it will be obvious, like the example above. Sometimes the decision will be made for you; a jockey, for example, must not weigh more than 8 stones/51 kg. Other times it will be less clear cut. A veterinary nurse could work for an animal welfare charity or a private veterinary surgery and still perform the same basic duties.

And while some careers offer new recruits on-the-job training and a chance to gain NVQs, others demand academic ability, proved through long periods at university. Vets, for example, need three A-levels at grades AAB just to be in the running for a place at veterinary college.

Most people start off by having an interest in a particular species and go on to turn their interest into a career. If you already know which animal you like best, choosing a career is made considerably easier.

But even within a species there are a number of related careers. Horse lovers could choose between racing, breeding, jumping, instruction, welfare, therapy or veterinary surgery. Dog lovers could choose between training, breeding, kennel work and racing, and then if they choose training, between pets, guide dogs, police dogs, army dogs and so on.

Some people choose an area of work instead, and begin to specialise later. Zoo keepers may already have a specialist knowledge but many will start off as volunteers and develop a keen interest in one particular species. The same is true of agriculture. While some farmers will know before they start training that they want to work with sheep or pigs or cows, others may choose while at agricultural college.

Nobody really knows why people develop an affinity for a particular species, but most people stick to one choice throughout their careers. This is partly because training is often biased towards one choice so that employees and employers get the best deal from any investment of time and money they make. One of the exceptions to this rule is veterinary surgery and nursing where trainees have to learn about the specific needs of a number of animals.

While many people crave a job working with animals, few who have experienced this rewarding work would swap it for any other. Although wages are generally lower and the work more physically demanding than in many other jobs, most people who work with animals would readily echo the words of this farm worker: 'You don't get drained doing this work. Exhausted, yes, but a healthy exhaustion'.

Anyone who thinks they want to work with animals should try it out first. Although surprisingly few are put off by the initial impression, if you aren't going to like certain aspects of the job it's best to find out sooner rather than later.

All animal work calls for some sort of vocation but this takes many forms. The desire to care for animals in trouble, which leads to nursing and charity work, is quite different from the instinct to control which is needed by trainers of show jumpers.

Vets may well be animal lovers, but their attitude to them is much like that of a good GP towards patients, emotionally detached. That is almost the opposite of the approach needed by a rider whose involvement with a horse is total.

Choosing which of the relationships suits you best is the key to finding the right job.

2 Vets

Introduction

While many youngsters would list becoming a vet as their first ambition, the high academic requirements, shortage of places and length of courses ensure that only a small proportion of these become qualified veterinary surgeons. The six universities which teach veterinary science – Bristol, Cambridge, Edinburgh, Glasgow, Liverpool and London – all demand A-level or Higher grades AAB in subjects such as chemistry, physics, biology, mathematics and zoology. Even then, an applicant with these grades may not get a place as only 400 students are accepted to train each year. Any would-be student should write to the universities, which are listed in Chapter 13, to find out what qualities and qualifications they are looking for. The Royal College of Veterinary Surgeons (RCVS) produces a free leaflet, *Training to be a Veterinary Surgeon*.

The veterinary schools' tradition of picking the brightest students has its critics, who feel it is bound to produce too many academics and not enough general practitioners. There is no doubt that it does exclude a few who might have made excellent working vets. However, it is unlikely to change, and it is defended by most qualified vets including one whose own 20-year-old son, who had three A-levels, was turned down. He said: 'This is a branch of medicine and standards have to be high. Vet schools have always produced a few academics, and who else would do the research and the teaching? But people who go to vet school wanting to be vets still want to be vets when they qualify.'

Case Study

One vet who excelled as a student is now in practice in Fife.

'My father was a vet and I grew up with the life. I always knew I would go into his practice one day. Certainly, nothing I experienced at vet school changed my mind, though it happened that I did quite well there. It is certainly the case that a professor will try to make an academic of a good student. My prof worked on me to stay on for another two years to do a BSc.

'Well, it's flattering, of course, and it can also make you wonder. I agreed at one point and did stay on for almost a year, but my heart wasn't in it.

'I had always wanted to be a working vet, doing what I'm doing now, so I left. I'm perfectly satisfied with my life. It is different perhaps in that I have become an expert in one particular species, and that has taken me round the world a bit, as adviser or giving technical evidence in disputes and court cases. But most of my life is spent here, about 50 per cent of my time with horses and cows belonging to local families I've known all my life. The rest of the work is with dogs and cats. You'll find few practices now, even in farm country, which don't handle small animals.

'I suppose the life is pretty much what you'd expect if you read James Herriot. I can't fault those books – in fact I wish I'd written them. The big difference, of course, is that they were set in the thirties, before reliable anaesthetics and, most important, before antibiotics. A vet's life in those respects is easier today. But have you noticed, when James Herriot went to a calving there was always a queue of people there, waiting to help? When I turn out there's a farmer with a bad back or something, and his wife who is just going to bed. But the routine *is* much the same, the same variety and triumphs and disasters.'

It is not, however, the life for all vets. There are over 14,000 in Britain and only 79 per cent of these work in private practice.

Case Study

Eileen is a vet in a Grimsby animal hospital. She has three nurses working for her whom she trained herself, and extremely well-equipped, modern working surroundings.

'I have worked in private practice, but I didn't particularly like it. The work I'm doing now is entirely with small animals, and I certainly find it just as interesting and fulfilling. It's a question of being practical. Who wants to go out in some mucky farmyard?

'It's much nicer to stay in a centrally heated building than to lie on your belly in the mud. No, I don't think this is anything to do with being female. There are a great many women vets, and I'm sure they can tackle any job the men can. A few, if they're on the small, dainty side, might need a hand – say with some cattle work. But if private practice appeals to them, they'll do it just as well as a male vet. It's a matter of personal preference.'

Thanks to research, there are constant developments and improvements in veterinary medicine. A busy practitioner *has* to keep up to date, but has difficulty in finding time for any of the innumerable refresher courses available. This is one reason why most vets now work in group practices. Another is the anti-social hours of the job.

Case Study

One West Country vet began on his own more than 20 years ago, and now shares a practice with three others.

'You can still stick your plate up and start off, but it would just about kill off a vet nowadays. A vet has to supply a 24-hour service. There has to be someone always on call, and when he's out there has to be someone to answer the telephone. No vet can count on a social life. You might invite your friends round for the evening, then arrive half-way through dripping of goodness knows what and smelling to high heaven.

'Even without emergencies, the hours are anti-social. Even in group practices, there's surgery three evenings a week until 7 pm and two or three nights a week on call.

'Different aspects of the work appeal more to some than others. In my practice routine surgery is done five mornings a week by one partner.

The sort of thing he's doing is spaying and castrating cats and dogs, and operating on accident victims and sick animals with tumours. There's a lot of work on teeth and ears. Now for some, this is the most interesting side of the work. To me everything is exciting the first dozen times.

'The first time you spay a cat – there's never been surgery like it! It's probably the first operation you've done entirely alone. No, you're not frightened. You're totally confident. It's the third or fourth time, when you know a bit more about it, that you're frightened.

'Veterinary work is a lot about people, and for me that is becoming more and more important and interesting. I'm a bit of a missionary about this. It may well be that when you see Mrs Bloggins' cat with the abscess for the tenth time it begins to lose its fascination – for the vet, but not for Mrs Bloggins. She's worried about her cat and she needs reassurance. There are hundreds of Mrs Blogginses. I feel it's a perfectly good use of veterinary time to reassure the humans. They're at least as important as the animals.'

Other prospects

The State Veterinary Service (SVS)

The State Veterinary Service is part of the Food Safety Directorate of the Department for Environment, Food and Rural Affairs (DEFRA). Vets appointed to the service (all jobs are advertised in the *Veterinary Record*) are called Veterinary Officers.

The Veterinary Field Service is responsible for controlling and eradicating notifiable animal diseases (including foot and mouth), monitoring the health of imported and exported animals, and promoting farm animal welfare. There are several regional offices with jurisdiction over smaller divisions. Each division has its own Animal Health Office, staffed by a team of veterinary officers, technical staff and support staff. Animal Health Divisional Officers are appointed to a division depending on their inclinations, aptitudes, and existence of vacancies.

Several other DEFRA agencies also employ vets. The Veterinary Laboratories Agency diagnoses diseased animals for private vets and for the Veterinary Field Service at its Veterinary Investigation Centres; the Veterinary Medicines Directorate is responsible for licensing veterinary medicines; and the Meat

Hygiene Service is responsible for enforcing public health regulations in slaughterhouses and other meat processing premises. Under the Meat Hygiene Regulations large plants have to employ a vet to make sure that animals are properly stunned, and killed humanely.

The Royal Army Veterinary Corps (RAVC) Veterinary Officer

Veterinary Officers working for the RAVC are first and foremost officers, with veterinary expertise. This means they have a command role. VOs are involved in every aspect of the use of animals in a military environment, from their procurement right through to their retirement from the service; they are responsible for the maintenance of the animals' health and fitness throughout their service life. VOs serve a minimum of four years, which can be extended to eight years or converted to a regular commission on suitable recommendation. You must be a qualified vet and a member of the RCVS to enter, but a small number of bursaries are given to outstanding students to help them through their studies. For more information contact the Regimental Secretary at the RAVC headquarters in Leicestershire.

Animal welfare

Many vets prefer hospital work and some are employed by animal welfare organisations, such as the PDSA which – as Britain's largest veterinary charity – employs over 220 veterinary surgeons. It is not necessary to have a special vocation for charitable work, although many vets clearly do. In terms of small animal practice experience the PDSA provides a wide range of opportunities. The standard of care provided matches that of a good-quality private practice. For more information see Chapter 4.

Case Study

Harry is a fourth-year veterinary student.

'I've just spent Christmas in practice in the north and thoroughly enjoyed it. I lived with one of the partners' family and that side of it was really great, especially New Year's Eve. You could tell just by looking round the room who was on call. It was my second spell in practice and you don't exactly lead a sheltered life at vet college, so I knew what to expect, but what I didn't reckon on was the cold.

'Farmers seem to be one extreme or the other. Some call in the vet because they are vaguely worried about an animal when it's much too soon to make a diagnosis. We had one like that and the senior partner turned to me, straight-faced, and said, 'What would *you* say, Harry?' Naturally I thought he had it all sussed out and I couldn't see a damn thing wrong with the brute. Others seem to wait until the animal is about to die, which is a bit depressing because by then it's too late to do much.

'In this practice there was a farmer whose panic level was pretty low. If he rang to say a cow was about to calve, the vet would say, 'Better get a move on or it will arrive without us and there will be no fee.' Most cows get on with it, without help, but about 5 per cent do need assistance. I've never been in on any of the dramatic midnight calvings by storm lantern so much loved in fiction. But I did go on a few night calls.

'There are four vets in that practice and they take night duty in turns, but a student is supposed to come on all enthusiastic and not miss a thing.

'Actually, to be quite serious, I wouldn't have missed any of it. But there was an hour or so, freezing in a pig shed, wearing someone else's gumboots which were giving me hell because my own were still soaked from the last call, when I asked myself if maybe I should be looking for a cushier job like, say, oil-rig drilling in the North Sea.'

Salaries

A newly qualified veterinary surgeon entering general practice as an assistant will receive around £15,500–£25,000 including car and accommodation, and a continued professional development allowance. Veterinary surgeons can earn between £23,000 and £29,000. Chief veterinary surgeons can earn between £35,000 and £40,000.

Qualities

The demands made by universities are understandable. The amount of academic work covered by them is formidable but, just like doctors, vets need other qualities more difficult to measure. All through their years of study they are coming into contact with live animals. Their training gears them to cure and prevent disease. The realities of practice call for a heavy blend of caring and detachment. The responsibilities they take on are a high price to pay for the lifestyle most of them will say is ideal.

3 Veterinary nurses

No vet could survive for long in practice without assistants. In the words of a 19-year-old who works in a London practice: 'There's a girl who keeps the records, a girl who makes appointments, a receptionist, a pre-op and a post-op nurse, and a girl who makes the tea. Me.'

In fact there are two trainee nurses in that practice and they both perform all the duties she described. They also help with X-rays, anaesthetics and sterilising of instruments and do a very large amount of cleaning up. They will learn about theatre work, ordering drugs, laboratory diagnostic tests, and the care and treatment of animal patients kept in the ward. They are training for qualification as Veterinary Nurses (VNs).

The British Veterinary Nursing Association (BVNA) controls training standards and anyone considering a career as a veterinary nurse should contact them first. On receipt of an sae they will send out their information pack. Alternatively, visit their Web site at www.bvna.org.uk.

Trainee Veterinary Nurses earn between £7,000 and £8,000 per annum depending on the practice and the region. On qualification this rises to £12,000–£15,000.

Qualifications

A trainee needs five A, B or C passes at GCSE/SCE, which must include English language and either a physical or a biological science or mathematics, or appropriate passes in examinations of a comparable or higher standard. If you do not have the appropriate qualifications it is still possible to take the BVNA's Pre-Veterinary Nursing Course which is the equivalent of four GCSE/SCE passes. Training takes a minimum of two years. An applicant must be at least 16 (there is no upper limit) and have been working in a veterinary practice for at least 9 months full time or 18 months part time. The course can be by distance learning or college attendance and you will be required to complete a practical assessment book and take a written examination.

Training

The first step is to find employment at an Approved Training and Assessment Centre (ATAC). Without this, or the promise in writing of such a job, no one can enrol with the Royal College of Veterinary Surgeons (RCVS) as a trainee. These centres are veterinary practices or animal centres, such as those run by the RSPCA, PDSA and the Blue Cross, which have been approved by the Royal College of Veterinary Surgeons. A list is available from the BVNA. (Please send a large stamped addressed envelope and a cheque for £2.00 to the BVNA.)

Posts for trainees are advertised weekly in the *Veterinary Record* (available from the British Veterinary Association), and in *Veterinary Nursing* (available from the BVNA).

Training extends over a minimum of two years and combines on the job training with college instruction. This leads to Scottish or National Vocational Qualifications at Levels 2 and 3. During your training you will undertake a broad range of veterinary nursing practice under supervision. Any college training will be arranged through your ATAC. You will be assessed in practice and will also take exams at the end of your first and second years. When you have completed your training you will be awarded the RCVS Veterinary Nursing Certificate. It is also possible to take an academic qualification in addition to practical training and a number of universities and colleges offer integrated degree or HND programmes.

Working for a local veterinary surgery on a voluntary basis gives a chance to get an idea of the duties of a veterinary nurse, and the experience can help in getting a full-time place.

Case Study

Kim is 20 and works for a practice in Hertfordshire.

'I wanted to be a vet, but I wasn't sure I wanted to stay on for my A-levels, so I decided to be a nurse.

'I did a bit of work with animals first, to find out if I was as keen as I thought, and I recommend that to anyone who is thinking of taking this up. I worked for eight months as a kennel maid, then applied for a place in an approved practice.

'The course is actually a small animals course, but the practice I'm with is mixed, dealing with horses, cows, pigs and sheep as well as cats and dogs, so my life is a lot more varied than most. I go out to farms with the vet. I also do a bit of reception work, give out drugs, answer telephones – I book appointments, making decisions about what is an emergency.

'We have a week on the ward, mainly post-operative care of patients, some with long-standing diseases. Sick animals can get a bit snappy but it doesn't bother me. If a dog is determined to have a go I'll bandage up its nose.

'I assist in ops, taking care of sterilising instruments, administering anaesthesia – and cleaning up. There's a lot of that and it gets very messy. Vomit, diarrhoea, blood – not for the squeamish.

'I am in my second year now and I earn about £50 a week [rates may be higher depending on the area you live in]. It's not marvellous, but I have free accommodation. In fact a lot of people leave because of the money. It means you have to be dependent on your parents and although I get on very well with mine I'd rather not have to ask them for money at my age. Still, I suppose if I had gone to veterinary college I'd be round their necks a lot longer. Because so many people want to do this job, vets don't have to pay more.

'I go to college once a week. The course covers anatomy and physiology of dogs, cats, birds – bones, muscles, nerves, liver, kidneys. I draw lots of lovely diagrams. Actually, I am enjoying the studying side. I even thought I might, after all, go on to try for vet college, but I decided I enjoy my job more.'

Case Study

Rosemary *is 22 and works as a receptionist for a vet in Essex.*

'I did a secretarial course and had quite a good job with a cosmetics firm for a year, but I was unsettled. It's the old story. I had always wanted to work with animals, but I knew I'd never stick all those years in college, so I gave up the idea. Then this job came up. It meant quite a drop in pay – I was earning a good salary in my old job. I was taken on as a receptionist and that's what I am, officially. I do work as a receptionist. We all do here, taking it in turns.

'There are four of us, two vet's assistants and two lay staff, but we all find ourselves helping out in odd ways. The duty vet might ask one to help hold an animal during surgery.

'I don't do any op work, although I help out with the cleaning up and sterilisation. The first time I asked to watch an operation I was a bit afraid I might blow it. It was a spaying – a lot of them are. There was quite a lot of blood and mess, but the strange thing is, I was too interested to feel sick or anything.

'The thing that upsets me is when an animal is put down. If an animal is ill or dying, then I can see it's the only merciful thing to do. But people bring healthy dogs and cats here, just to get them out of the way. The vets I work for have a policy of refusing to put down a healthy animal, but you'd be surprised how many people ask. I suppose it's better than chucking them out to fend for themselves, but there's a look about those animals, and it's not just my imagination, that really breaks me up.'

---

4 Animal welfare and conservation charities

Animals throughout the world are cared for and protected by charities. Wild, domestic and farm animals which are deserted, neglected, ill-treated or tortured often die in misery. The lucky ones make it to an animal hospital or sanctuary. Wild animals face multiple threats, from hunting and trade to pollution and the destruction of their habitats.

While the need for animal care is great, the funds available to charities are not. With limited commercial opportunities most animal welfare charities survive by employing a mixture of paid staff and volunteers. For volunteers this is not necessarily a bad thing. Volunteering provides a valuable opportunity to get work experience and meet potential employers.

For some, animal welfare work is the only option. Many of the organisations listed in the *Animal Contacts Directory 2001/2* (available from Veggies Catering Campaign, price £4.95) were started by single-minded individuals dedicated to the protection of a particular species or type of animal. It is their vocation because the rewards of their work are the animals that go on to lead happier lives.

For many animals such help comes too late. Anyone thinking of taking up a job in animal welfare should be prepared for the sad days.

Royal Society for the Prevention of Cruelty to Animals (RSPCA)

The RSPCA is the biggest animal charity. It operates 42 clinics, 10 welfare centres, four hospitals, three wildlife hospitals, and 52 animal centres. As well as 328 inspectors, it employs kennel assistants, hospital and clinic assistants, vets and veterinary nurses and is approved for VN training. In addition, it employs education officers, wildlife, farm and animal research experts, press officers, journalists and administrators. For those with an interest in animal welfare but lacking the skills associated with hands-on animal care, these are options well worth considering. The RSPCA runs three wildlife hospitals, one at Taunton, one in Norfolk and one in Cheshire.

Like most charities, the RSPCA welcomes voluntary help in some areas and does employ school-leavers.

At the headquarters in Horsham a spokesman said: 'A lot of young people are perhaps a bit idealistic when they come to us, which can be a good thing if they have their eyes open about the work. Most of them do, but there are stumbling blocks. One of these, of course, is euthanasia. Every year about 70,000 animals have to be destroyed. They are kept for as long as possible, and finding homes for them is our first priority. If there is very little chance of rehoming, if the animal is temperamentally unsuitable, or too old, or – and it's hard to say this – too unattractive, then it has to be put down.'

Hospital and clinic assistants work in the RSPCA hospitals. Applicants must be at least 18 and live near the hospital as the job is non-residential. Training is given for six months on full pay, with instruction given under the supervision of a veterinary surgeon on animal first-aid, euthanasia, clinic hygiene and general reception work.

Kennel assistants are involved with kennel hygiene, animal first-aid, routine exercising, cleaning and grooming. Some aspects of the job are distressing but it can also be very rewarding.

Vacancies for full-time paid employees are limited, as most animal homes are staffed by voluntary workers.

Candidates for inspector should be aged between 22 and 40, have a good general education, physical fitness and hold a clean driving licence. The five- to six-month training period covers theoretical and field training and includes a final examination. Inspectors must be willing to serve anywhere in England and Wales.

Routine

Whatever their history and whatever their fate, animals in RSPCA care need exactly the same attention as animals in kennels anywhere. At one animal home, in Surrey, a senior staff member said: 'We do get young people coming to work here who want to mollycoddle the dogs, thinking the work here is all grooming and walking and tender loving care. Well, they do need a lot of that, of course. Some of them come in starving and frightened, so they're not like the boarding kennel dogs and cats in that sense.

'What I would warn a youngster hoping for this work about is that you do get disillusioned. These beginners are animal lovers and they just don't realise the way people treat their so-called pets. When people come wanting a dog, you really question them. You have to know why they want it and whether they can keep it properly. Sometimes they're looking for status symbols. You do get people in a one-bedroomed flat looking for a Great Dane. You have to be sure that the whole family wants the animal, that it will get the exercise it needs, that it will be properly fed. You can tell a lot by the answers people give. And yes, we do often turn people down.

'You've got to do that tactfully, of course. I usually get round it by saying the Inspector will have to call first and see the home. Then I leave it to the Inspector.'

Case Study

Basil is an RSPCA inspector.

'Ever since childhood I wanted to work with animals. There is residential training at the RSPCA College, which is very intensive, dealing with law, lectures from vets, every aspect of the work.

'It's hard to generalise about this job because every day is different. One is dealing with animals and people. So much of the work is inspecting complaints of cruelty. Around 100,000 are made each year throughout the country.

'Most of the complaints are from people genuinely concerned, but 75 per cent of them are unfounded. If an animal is being mistreated or cruelly treated, one feels a controlled anger. You have to feel this anger. There would be no point if you didn't care. But actually there is more ignorance than cruelty. Things are getting worse, with the recession and unemployment. People aren't taking animals to the vet, to avoid fees, and perhaps they cut down on food. It all contributes to neglect.

'The thing to remember is that we are not a punitive organisation. We are offering a public service. Most of the time is spent advising and helping. Very few cases of cruelty come before the courts. What is frustrating is that we have no power to remove an animal, however bad the conditions, unless the owner legally signs it over. We can caution people and take statements, then Headquarters takes over, proceeding through the courts if necessary.

'People are not always as shocked as you might think by a visit from an RSPCA inspector. Some are very belligerent and aggressive or arrogant. It is not a job for a timid person. You're faced with heart-breaking options. Yesterday I had to put a boxer dog to sleep. It was nearly blind, very old and lame, and I know it was right, but the fact remains: yesterday I put down a boxer.

'We inspect pet shops, all boarding establishments, riding schools and are welcomed in 75 per cent of cases. We have a good relationship with most pet shops, but some are frankly shady – illegally caught finches, that sort of thing. We visit street markets and you need eyes in the back of your head. Deals go on in back streets and we are very conscious of our limited power. We do wear a uniform. I often think we'd do better in jeans with a two-day growth of beard, but we do have a public image.

'You need to be a bit of a detective and a bit of a diplomat. You must be able to communicate with people. And you must have a great love and concern for animals and really love the job; otherwise you wouldn't stay. The salary is not high. You need a genuine vocation, and if you've got it, you know you've got it.'

Scottish Society for the Prevention of Cruelty to Animals (SSPCA)

The SSPCA performs the same function as the RSPCA in Scotland. Competition for places however is fierce. Although they receive 50–60 applications per week the SSPCA can only offer two vacancies per year. Thus applicants will be exceptional individuals with substantial previous experience of working with animals (preferably from a farm or veterinary background). The minimum age of entry for training as an Inspector is 25; the upper age limit is 45. Training lasts five months and is split between the Edinburgh headquarters and field work. Probationary Inspectors earn £12,466 per year, rising to about £17,000 once qualified.

People's Dispensary for Sick Animals (PDSA)

The PDSA was founded in 1917 to provide free treatment for animals of people who could not afford private veterinary fees. Today its services are available to pet owners in receipt of certain state benefits including Housing Benefit and Council Tax Benefit. PDSA PetAid is a network of purpose-built animal hospitals and private practices that provide care for sick and injured pets of eligible owners from Aberdeen to Plymouth.

As Britain's largest veterinary charity it employs around 220 vets and 280 qualified nurses. The student veterinary nurse trains over a minimum of two years with two examinations in that period. Once the student has passed the Part Two examination he or she may apply for inclusion in the RCVS list of veterinary nurses and is entitled to use the letters VN after his/her name.

Salaries

The salaries for PDSA VNs range from £6,924 a year for student nurses to £12,806 for qualified VNs at the top of the incremental scale.

Other employment opportunities

Increasingly, PDSA hospitals employ animal care auxiliaries on varying shift rotas, but mainly at night, caring for inpatients, assisting with out-of-hours emergency treatment, security and cleaning. PDSA hospitals also employ part-time receptionists. The work involves dealing with the public in person and by telephone and undertaking associated clerical duties.

The Blue Cross

The Blue Cross (incorporating Our Dumb Friends' League) was founded in 1897. During the First World War the Red Cross saved human casualties, The Blue Cross saved horses. Today there are more than 300 staff employed by The Blue Cross – at eleven adoption centres, two equine centres, and four animal hospitals. In addition, The Irish Blue Cross operates a mobile clinic service.

The work of The Blue Cross includes housing, rehabilitating and rehoming animals; offering professional guidance on animal behavioural problems (see page 49 for careers as an animal behaviourist); encouraging responsible pet ownership; and providing veterinary consultations and operations for owners who cannot afford the cost of treatment. The Blue Cross operates a Horse Ambulance Service that attends horse trials and other special events. In association with the Society for Companion Animal Studies (SCAS), The Blue Cross also runs the National Pet Bereavement Service using a network of volunteers to help people who have lost a companion animal through death or enforced separation.

All staff members must follow The Blue Cross pledge: 'every animal has the right to be treated with kindness and respect; every animal in pain has the right to proper veterinary care; every abandoned animal has the right to a loving, caring home; and no healthy animal should ever be destroyed simply for want of a home'.

Not all animals come to The Blue Cross because they are in the care of abusive owners; sometimes owners simply do not know how to care for their pets. Others need pets to overcome loneliness but struggle on low incomes. Some animals come to The Blue Cross because their owner has died, gone through a divorce or even redundancy. One staff member described how this can be particularly tragic: 'One chap came in with tears running down his face because he could not afford to keep his dog. It was a really superb Alsatian and they thought the world of each other. But he had just been made redundant. That kind of thing is very sad, and, of course, no one can explain it to the dog'.

Animal conservation

Animal conservation work can offer close contact with animals that are both amazing and beautiful but much of the work is creating, protecting or maintaining the right sort of habitat. Finding work in this area is not easy. Most people start off by developing their interest in conservation by volunteering. A large number of conservation organisations take on volunteers. (See Chapter 14, Useful addresses and Chapter 15, Further reading.)

Royal Society for the Protection of Birds (RSPB)

The Royal Society for the Protection of Birds currently runs 150 reserves in Britain. It employs permanent wardens, permanent assistant wardens and in the summer temporary assistant wardens to help with visitors as well as the usual work of the site. Much of the work involves preparing suitable habitats for the birds, and physical tasks such as thinning scrub, cutting reeds and clearing ditches are common. Wardens must have excellent ornithological knowledge, being able to identify birds, maintain accurate records and write up regular reports. The RSPB does not care for sick and injured birds; they would be referred to the RSPCA.

From the age of 16 you can apply to become a voluntary warden and duties may include escorting visitors, keeping records of birds and carrying out physical work. From the age of 20 you can apply to be a summer warden. The jobs are usually advertised in the RSPB magazine *Birds*. Long working hours are par for the course and applicants must enjoy meeting people and be prepared to undertake physical work.

The most outstanding summer wardens might have the opportunity to become permanent assistant wardens or permanent wardens but competition is fierce and demand for places always outstrips supply. In addition, there are a number of opportunities to work at the Society's headquarters at The Lodge in Sandy, Bedfordshire.

Animal sanctuaries

There are a number of animal sanctuaries, some of which offer paid or voluntary work. Sanctuaries usually protect one species or type of animal; these include owls, hedgehogs, guinea pigs, foxes, horses, donkeys, monkeys and oil-spill victims. Each should be contacted individually. The following is one example.

The Monkey Sanctuary

The Monkey Sanctuary was established in 1964 to provide a stable setting in which woolly monkeys, rescued from lives of isolation in zoos or as pets, could live as naturally as possible, in a colony. The care of the monkeys is in the hands of a highly experienced team of people.

The keeper's work includes caring for the monkeys' health and environment and day-to-day well-being, as well as passing on these skills to future team members. When permanent team members are required at the Sanctuary, people are more likely to be selected if they have come to know the monkeys, the team and the lifestyle through being there as volunteers.

Volunteers stay for periods of two to several weeks depending on demand and in exchange for their help they live in with the Sanctuary team. No qualifications are needed but a concern for animal welfare and conservation is. In the summer, work is geared more specifically around receiving visitors, so if specific conservation or maintenance work is more your thing, the autumn and winter is the better time to volunteer. Write to The Monkey Sanctuary for more information.

5 Working with horses

Stable lads

Stable lads, a name given to men and women, start off by performing the most menial tasks. Work starts early with mucking out. Horses are brushed, yards swept, and tack (saddles, harnesses, bridles) cleaned. Water has to be checked, straw changed and hay fetched. Mash has to be mixed up for three feeds, and other food cleaned and chopped.

A stable lad will also accompany horses to the vet or perform road work, a difficult and hazardous task which can result in riders falling off. To move on from basic work or to be trusted to ride the horse most prized by the stables, lads will have to prove themselves to the head lad, who makes all the day-to-day decisions. Progress is gradual, standards strict and at the end of years of hard work, few become successful jockeys.

Training for stable lads is given by private trainers and at the British Racing School and the Northern Racing College.

A list of trainers (over 500 in the British Isles) is given in *Horses in Training*, which can be bought from bookshops and is also in most libraries. Job applications can be made direct to a trainer. *Racing Post* and *Horse and Hound* may also carry job advertisements. Many trainers take on school leavers on National Traineeship and Modern Apprenticeship programmes. Experience is necessary before trying to work in a racing yard as trainers do not normally have time to teach complete beginners. To work as a stable lad in flat-racing yards you should weigh less than 9½ stone (60 kg).

Previous experience is not essential before applying for the courses at the two racing schools.

The training programme is on the lines of a real racing stable with instruction on riding, grooming, feeding, mucking out and lectures on the parts of a horse, its health, possible ailments, lameness etc. The courses are open to 16–19-year-olds and satisfactory trainees are guaranteed jobs in racing yards. Trainees should have good eyesight without glasses, no chest complaints or asthma. Good exam results are not essential but applicants must be alert, quick to learn and able to read and write. Training, accommodation and food are free.

The courses at the schools lead to National Vocational Qualifications (NVQs) in Racehorse Care and Management up to level 3.

A few stable lad trainers do go on to become jockeys, but out of 4,500 stable staff, only 200 are professional jockeys; those who do not become jockeys can become head lad, or a travelling head lad or assistant trainer, or even eventually make it to trainer.

Would-be flat race jockeys are apprenticed to a trainer for a period between the ages of 16 and 20, working as stable lads and riding in races if they are good enough. Steeplechase, or 'jump', jockeys do not have any formal training, but are apprenticed as 'conditional jockeys' up to the age of 25, with instruction being given by the trainer. There are also several courses each year for apprentice jockeys at the British Racing School. Sixteen-year-olds who want to be jockeys on the flat must not weigh more than 7–8 stone (44–51 kg); the limit for jump jockeys is around 8–9 stone (51–57 kg). Often jump jockeys are ex-flat race jockeys who have grown too heavy, or who have been riding previously in point-to-point races.

For more information, contact the British Horseracing Training Board (BHTB).

Pay

Low pay is legendary. The minimum rate of pay for a 40-hour week, including overtime, varies between £102.86 for a lad aged 16 to £164.00 for a lad who has completed NVQ level 2 with 18 months' experience in a racing yard.

Stud work

The stud year has three separate phases. The busiest time for the stable staff is from February to June, which is the breeding season. The months from July to October are less busy, with the most important work being to prepare the yearlings for the autumn sales. November to January is the time for routine maintenance and for taking holidays.

Stud workers are paid according to experience; wages are normally higher than the minimum agricultural wage. Opportunities for promotion are limited, but the positions of stallion men or stud grooms carry higher salaries for extra responsibilities.

Formal qualifications are not required but some experience of handling thoroughbred horses is preferred, together with some knowledge of stable management and general horse care. Someone under 19 years of age can enter the industry as a trainee stud hand via the British Stud Staff Training Scheme. Alternatively, they can write to the Thoroughbred Breeders Association which has a list of studs willing to take on trainee stud hands; to studs (their addresses can be found in the *Directory of Turf*); or use the situations vacant columns in the racing papers.

Stud workers usually work towards NVQ qualifications in Racehorse Care and Management while they are employed but it is possible to take a college based vocational course such as the highly regarded one- and two-year courses in Stud and Stable Husbandry offered at the West Oxfordshire College of Witney and The National Stud's intensive National Stud Diploma. The Thoroughbred Breeders Association will send out a list of horse-related courses and the colleges which offer them if they receive a large sae with 38p in stamps.

The National Pony Society offers the Stud Assistant's Certificate and the NPS Diploma (non-riding) in Pony Mastership and Breeding. The Society publishes a list of training establishments in stud work; trainees can take the NVQ in Horse Care and Management Levels 1, 2 and 3.

Show jumping

For many show jumping fans, the peak of ambition is to act as groom to one of the competitors. While many treat grooms well and pay them fairly, this is an area of great exploitation. One regular eventer said: 'Frankly, this is an expensive business and I'm sorry to say there are people who exploit these young-sters. It's regarded as one of the little economies. There are so many keen youngsters, queuing up for jobs, hanging around at events. They want to get into the world of eventing and show jumping and I suppose this is one way to do it.'

Case Study

Lisa *is a groom and qualified instructor.*

'You can find yourself sleeping in the stockman's tent, huts, all sorts of places, travelling all over Britain. Mind you, you can get it cushy. But I wouldn't recommend it to someone young. You've got to be a very good rider and know all there is to know about looking after a horse. Some eventers won't let anyone exercise their horse. But many do, and you can come off. That's when you discover your employer doesn't believe in buying insurance stamps – a not uncommon occurrence, believe me.'

Riding schools

Every year hundreds seek jobs in riding schools for a year (September to August), hoping to become instructors. If they can afford it they pay for intensive instruction. Talland School of Equitation in Cirencester is one of the riding schools offering this sort of training. Approved by the British Horse Society (BHS) and the Association of British Riding Schools (ABRS), it offers a variety of options for trainees, lasting from 17 weeks to a year. All prices include full-board accommodation and tuition but trainees are expected to do stable work as well. Students pay £270 a week for 17 weeks, £130 a week for 24 weeks or £115 a week for a year. For details of other courses contact the BHS.

It was once possible to work in exchange for training but the introduction of the National Minimum Wage (NMW) has put an end to this – although there are some exemptions: workers under the age of 18; workers under 26 who are in the first year of their Modern Apprenticeship or 'Contract of Apprentice-ship'; and workers who are attending work experience, not exceeding one year, as a required part of a higher education course. All other workers receive a set hourly wage of £3.20 if aged between 18–21 and £3.70 for everyone else over 22 (although both these figures are set to rise in October 2001). A riding centre can be fined for not paying the right rates so if you have any doubts, contact the BHS.

Case Study

Angela runs a riding school in Suffolk. Her stables are approved by the British Horse Society, which carries out regular inspections of all its listed establishments.

'My advice to anyone looking for work in stables is to write to the Society. It seems an obvious first step, yet so many people don't do it. There is a lot of ignorance, or innocence, on the part of both youngsters and their parents. I advise them to have a written contract with their employer, setting out hours of work, time off and conditions. It should be read by parents, with a solicitor's advice if necessary. And everyone should find out if there will be insurance cover. Quite often there will not. I know of one case where a girl came off a horse very badly. The fall was entirely due to a broken bridle. She was laid up for weeks without pay. And when she returned, the owner charged her for the broken bridle.'

It is not unusual for people to find after starting that they do not want to become instructors after all. If they have learnt enough about horse care, including treatment of minor ailments, stable management and routine, and have good riding ability, they can still achieve qualifications and find satisfying work in stables. They can sit for the BHS examinations (see below) or the Association of British Riding Schools' Preliminary Groom's Certificate, Groom's Certificate and Groom's Diploma.

British Horse Society (BHS)

The BHS holds examinations at centres throughout the country, to give qualifications for a career working with horses. There is a comprehensive syllabus that includes horse care as well as riding.

Many options are open, especially for those who intend to look after horses rather than to ride them. It is possible to climb up a ladder of advanced qualifications but all trainees start by learning the basics. The first stage, the British Horse Society Assistant Instructor (BHSAI) Certificate, is offered under Trainee Schemes but the more advanced qualifications would be taken after 18. These are the Intermediate Instructor's Certificate, the Instructor's Certificate, the Stable Manager's Certificate and the Fellowship of the British Horse Society. The BHSAI course includes components on horse physiology and psychology, health, management, general handling, feeding, sick horses and general knowledge subjects such as insurance. Syllabuses for all the BHS examinations are available from the BHS (30p each plus sae).

The BHS produces a book, *Where to Ride*, which gives information on riding establishments which are approved as places of training. It is available from large bookshops or from the BHS Approvals Office (£5.95 including postage and packing). Most of the approved establishments that offer careers training can offer working student or fee-paying places.

Courses

A great many courses exist at colleges throughout the country (see pages 79–89). Contact the British Horse Society for further details of examinations and courses, including the BSc (Hons) in Equine Sports Coaching – developed in conjunction with University College Worcester.

National Vocational Qualifications/Scottish Vocational Qualifications

The British Horse Society has been accredited by QCA and SQA as an awarding body for these awards, with approval from Lantra who are the National Training Organisation for the Equine Industry.

Candidates must register through an approved centre – which is an administrative centre – and will be assessed at an approved location linked to the centre. Centres will be responsible not only for the registration and maintenance of the progress records of candidates, but also for ensuring that adequate numbers of trained Assessors and Internal Verifiers are available. Candidates are assessed over a period of time and will be awarded the qualification when they have been assessed and verified, as being at the required standard for all the mandatory units, including one optional unit at Level 2 and 3. Unit certification is available for candidates who wish to complete individual units, or are unable to complete the full award.

The standards cover a wide variety of stable management tasks and routines including units involving health and safety requirements. The optional units at Level 2 and 3 include: breeding; exercising horses; schooling horses; driving; working heavy horses; trekking; care of performance horses; assisting riders with special needs (Level 2 only); polo; breaking; competition groom and coaching riders.

Copies of the full standards are available from the BHS at a cost of £1.50 for Level 1, £2.50 for Level 2 and £5.00 for Level 3, or free of charge via e-mail from exams@bhs.org.uk. A list of BHS accredited centres is available from the S/NVQ Administrator at the British Horse Society.

Modern Apprenticeship and National Traineeship

These two schemes are likely to become *the* work-based training programmes for future senior equine staff. For further information turn to page 77 or contact Lantra.

Association of British Riding Schools (ABRS)

The ABRS has a career and examination structure for grooms starting with the ABRS Preliminary Horse Care and Riding Certificate which is offered to trainees and other young persons involved in a career with horses. The ABRS Groom's Certificate is intended to provide a guide to employers in the selection of competent grooms. The holders, while capable of working on their own for a limited time, still require some supervision. The ABRS Groom's Diploma indicates that the holder is a competent groom who is capable not only of working on his or her own, but of organising the work of other staff. An experienced diploma holder is considered to be stable manager material. No GCSE passes are required for any of the ABRS examinations. There are also three teaching qualifications – The Initial Teaching Awards, The Teaching Certificate and The Advanced Teaching Diploma. Details of syllabuses can be obtained from the ABRS secretary, and the Association has a list of approved establishments which can offer training for their examinations. A list of establishments is also available from the British Horse Society.

Farriers

Farriery, or the shoeing of horses and similar animals, is an ancient craft. A farrier is a skilled craftsperson with a sound knowledge of both theory and practice of the craft, capable of shoeing all types of feet, whether normal or defective, of making shoes to suit all types of work and working conditions, and of devising corrective measures to compensate for faulty limb action. Farriery is hard work, especially as some animals can be fractious, but it is also an individual handcraft from which intense satisfaction may be derived.

Apprenticeships

To practise, farriers must be registered by the Farriers Registration Council into the Register of Farriers. Apprentices can only practise farriery under formal Articles of Apprenticeship to an Approved Training Farrier (ATF). An ATF is a farrier who has completed the ATF course and made a successful application to the Registration Committee of the Farriers Registration Council for approval as a training farrier.

Responsibility for recruitment and selection of apprentices lies with individual ATFs who have a clear idea of their own requirements and the needs of young people entering farriery. In particular, they will seek evidence to demonstrate that the applicant is capable of completing the course of training. Care should be taken that young people have realistic expectations of the nature of employment within the sector – idyllic stereotypes seldom last long.

During the course of training the following items must be successfully completed in the specified order:

1. All mandatory college assessments
2. NVQ Level 3 in Farriery
3. Farriery Modern Apprenticeship requirements including key skills
4. Diploma of the Worshipful Company of Farriers Examination
5. The period of training prescribed by the Farriers Registration Council (currently four years and two months).

Training comprises planned experience gained with an Approved Training Farrier, interspersed with periods of centralised off-the-job training totalling 23 weeks at an approved college.

Candidates for a Modern Apprenticeship in Farriery must be at least 16 years of age. There is no upper age limit. Prior to the commencement of an Apprenticeship, candidates are required to undergo a medical examination (at their own expense) which must include a test for colour blindness, although this is not a hindrance to applicants. The minimum requirements for entry are four GCSEs at grade C or above, including English language, or successful completion of the entrance examination.

This is a written paper testing basic English, maths and graphic skills and lasts approximately one hour.

The Apprenticeship costs £5,750 – payable in half-yearly instalments – and grant aid may be available for those who will be aged under 26½ by the end of training. Anyone older than this will have to bear the full cost. Anyone wanting further details of the Farriery Apprenticeship Scheme should send £5 to The Farriery Training Service for their *Guide to Modern Apprenticeships in Farriery* and a list of Approved Training Farriers.

Pay

There is no set wage for qualified farriers and their income depends to a large extent on the amount of work the individual farrier is able to command, quality of work and competition for work in their area. For those under formal Articles of Apprenticeship, wages are set by the Farriers Registration Council for anyone outside of the National Minimum Wage legislation.

The Armed Services

The King's Troop Royal Horse Artillery

The Troop is seen every summer pulling the guns during the musical drive in the Royal Tournament. It is also responsible for the firing of royal salutes in Hyde Park in London on special occasions, such as royal anniversaries and state ceremonies. The Artillery is the branch of the army responsible for guns and missiles.

New recruits do not have to be able to ride. There are Monday to Friday courses every month (except during the Royal Tournament in July) when about six potential recruits are given the chance to find out if they would be suitable; the course includes riding instruction. If they are interested in joining the Troop, they must then go through normal army selection procedures. Those who are not skilled enough to ride on parade and in the Royal Tournament may become limber gunners or stablemen responsible for the care of the horses. All get a chance to ride out on exercise and each man has his own horses in his charge in the stables. Members of the Troop include farriers and saddlers, and everyone learns to ride – including tailors, storemen, vehicle drivers and batmen.

Mounted dutymen in the Household Cavalry

The Household Cavalry is an armoured regiment using tanks whose soldiers may be crewmen, drivers or mounted dutymen. They provide the Queen's Life Guard at Horse Guards Parade and carry out duties for the royal family and visiting heads of state. Like the King's Troop Royal Horse Artillery, the regiment includes farriers and saddlers.

Mounted police

Horses in the police service have a far greater role than those used for ceremonial duties in the armed services. Riders are very skilled and horse and rider play a vital role at events where there are large crowds, such as football matches, race meetings and demonstrations. Not all forces have a mounted section, and in those that do the branch is usually quite small and the opportunities for promotion are limited.

An officer must complete two years' foot duty before applying for a post in the mounted branch to ensure that he or she is well grounded in general police work.

The majority of recruits in the Metropolitan Police have no previous experience of working with horses, but this is not always the case in the smaller forces. However, no one should consider lack of experience a bar to this work because all recruits take a 16-week riding and equine course. The course covers theory and practice and is the same for whichever force you join. Recruiting officers are looking for people who are good police officers first and foremost. Although police officers can apply for the mounted police units after two years of service most officers don't make it that quickly. It is possible to serve on the force for twenty years before joining a mounted unit.

The officer on the beat is sent out to prevent and detect crime, and this includes the more mundane offences – such as driving without a vehicle tax disc or seat belt. An average day (or night) includes a four-hour patrol – which can include watching over pubs and clubs until four or five in the morning – paperwork and routine station duties. Police officers no longer groom their horses as civilians fulfil this role. About 10 per cent of a mounted police officer's time is spent attending special events, demonstrations and sporting fixtures, but this will depend on the force you join. Not all forces have a mounted unit, and those that don't, hire a unit when they need one. There are 14 in England and Wales, two in Scotland and one in Ireland. There is also the Royal Parks Police, seen escorting the changing of the guards at Buckingham Palace.

For further information contact the recruitment officer of your chosen police force.

6 Working with dogs

Dogs are quite often not only man's best friend, but man's life-line, living or protector. The various occupations in this chapter include guide dog trainer, police dog handler, kennel hand and general dog trainer.

Kennel work

Although there are a great many private training courses for all aspects of dog care, most kennel owners prefer to employ people straight from school. One owner said he likes people to come to work for him before they have softened up in an indoor job. The work is largely outdoors, starts early in the morning and is physically very demanding.

Kennel work is not particularly well paid and varies, depending on the region you live in and the type of accommodation arrangement that goes with the job. This can range from a room in a house, to a flat or a caravan. Quite often food is provided and junior kennel staff may live as part of the family unit, sharing cooking and eating arrangements.

Up until the introduction of the National Minimum Wage (NMW) pay rates for kennel hands were very poor indeed. All workers aged between 18 and 21 now receive an hourly wage of at least £3.20 and those over 22 get a minimum of £3.70 an hour. Unfortunately the NMW does not apply to under 18s, nor to people on the first year of a Modern Apprenticeship scheme or 'Contract of Apprenticeship'. Senior staff members with greater responsibility can expect around £200 a week. Even in the best-run establishments, where staff have proper working hours and adequate time off, the work is exhausting. However, skilled staff are in short supply, so those in their early twenties often find themselves with responsible jobs in management positions.

There are several different types of kennel to choose from: breeding, boarding, greyhound racing and those maintained by animal welfare organisations being the most numerous. There are also some opportunities in the Armed Forces.

Case Study

John Hyde owns the Star Boarding Kennels in Chessington.

'They come along, full of willingness and spirit, these young beginners, and for ten days they keep up the pace. Then they either pack it in, or slow right down. They wander about in a daze, knocked out by sheer hard work.

'That period can last for anything up to three weeks. Our senior staff are very experienced and they know the symptoms. They are pretty understanding. If the beginners come through that, they'll do. In my experience about three or four out of, say, 30 do come through it. They're usually girls.

'Anyone who comes along thinking they'll spend their time stroking lovely little cats and dogs all day has the wrong idea. Very few who come here for a job have any notion of the amount of work involved. Seventy per cent of it involves keeping the animals absolutely immaculate, cleaning bedding and runs, disinfecting and grooming. It starts at 7 am and the first break in the day comes at 11 am or 12. It's a five-day week, but that includes weekends and Christmas, which means shift work. You can't just fold animals up and put them in a filing cabinet at weekends. But we don't work our staff to death as some kennels do.'

Standards

Like all owners, Mr Hyde is ready to concede that there are a lot of badly run kennels. Some are too inefficient to provide much in the way of training for a beginner. Some are understaffed and ask a great deal too much from the workers they have.

How can an outsider looking for a job tell the good from the bad? One short, perfectly serious answer we were given to that question was: 'Use your nose.' A well-run kennels smells clean. A badly run one usually does not. The dogs themselves are the best advertisement for a good establishment. It does not take an expert to tell the difference between lively, properly fed creatures who are exercised regularly, and depressed, badly fed dogs who spend much too much time in unhygienic cages.

Training

Training is usually given on the job but there are also some full-time and part-time college courses. These lead to NVQs/SVQs Levels 1 and 2 in Animal Care, and the BTEC National Diploma in Animal Care. Trainees can combine practical work with a correspondence course to gain the National Small Animal Care Certificate. The course is run by the Animal Care College and Canine Studies Institute and is designed for trainees at boarding, quarantine, breeding, rescue and sanctuary kennels and is adaptable for use at pet shops and grooming establishments.

Case Study

Lynn is 24 and a senior kennel hand. She has been working in kennels since she was 14.

'I used to come here at holidays and weekends. You couldn't keep me away. The pay was low but that didn't bother me. It was the dogs I was interested in. I used to clean out kennels, walk the boarders, learn to groom, and I couldn't wait to come back each time. It never occurred to me there might be a dog I couldn't get on with. I do love dogs, but I'm not sentimental about them. I try to understand the way they think, what's going on in those furry minds. You have to, believe me. Actually, I have noticed a change in dogs over the years. Maybe it's due to inbreeding. Maybe people are bringing them up the wrong way. But years ago you never saw a neurotic retriever.

'You start as a kennel maid, cleaning out, answering the telephone, looking after the puppies. I still clean out. Everyone has to do that and it can come as a shock to beginners. You show them how to do it, make sure they're doing it properly, teach them the rules. Then you should be able to trust them to get on with it. But I've got a little lad here, and he needs watching. He'll skimp the job if he thinks he can get away with it. To be honest, I really can't understand that. If you like dogs and you want to work with them you've got to ask yourself, now what can I do to make this dog feel comfortable? Is the bed clean and dry? Is the water bowl clean? Is it empty? You don't do it because there's someone on your tail, you do it from affection for animals. And if you've got that, you won't think of the mucky side as boring.'

National Canine Defence League (NCDL)

Founded in 1891 to protect dogs from 'torture and ill-usage of every kind', the NCDL has combined campaigning with practical welfare for well over a century. Responsible for the introduction of several important animal welfare laws, it has helped to change the way we treat animals in this country; it now boasts over 500,000 supporters. The first NCDL clinic, offering free treatment, opened in Bethnal Green in 1926. By 1939 there were nine across London, dealing with over 80,000 animal patients a year. Today the NCDL cares for over 11,000 dogs every year in 16 rehoming centres throughout the UK. A non-destruction policy was adopted in 1964 and today, dogs that cannot be rehomed for some reason can be sponsored and become permanent residents. The NCDL offers a number of opportunities from day-to-day management to intensive canine care; job titles include Canine Carer, Training and Behaviour Advisor (TBA) and Rehoming Centre Manager. The NCDL always needs volunteers and opportunities include dog walking and dog socialising. A full list of training centres is available from the NCDL.

Dog warden

Usually employed by the local authority, the dog warden retrieves stray dogs and cares for them in the local authority kennel. If not reclaimed within one week they are rehomed or put down. The job may include educating the general public on responsible dog ownership and liaising with animal welfare organisations on neutering/microchipping initiatives. Dog wardens are 18 or over and must possess a full UK driving licence. Training is on the job. For further information contact the National Dog Wardens Association and the Woodgreen College of Animal Welfare.

Dog training

Training usually starts off as a part-time interest. Those who consider it their vocation are the ones who have the dedication and determination to turn their hobby into a full-time job. It is also possible to get work experience before becoming a full-time trainee trainer, as one owner of a dog training centre explained:

Case Study

Brian is the owner of a dog training centre.

'I prefer to take on school leavers here. Usually they come to us while still at school, for a week. At the end of that, if they are interested and we find their work satisfactory, we suggest they come at weekends. They are fully paid for any work they do during that time. I do not believe in making a profit out of someone's enthusiasm.

'Beginners are taught every aspect of kennel work, maintenance and dog care. It is physically demanding work, but everyone here shares it. We encourage animal husbandry training, giving the learners the chance to work with a veterinary surgery to increase their experience. Actually, it works in reverse too. Vets send their nurses to us during training. They begin dog training after a few months. This is a skill which can be acquired. The unskilled trainee does, after all, represent the general public who own these dogs and to whom these dogs will return. They need to have assurance with the dogs, and that too can be acquired.'

Many trainers work alone, specialising in training gun dogs, greyhounds, guard dogs or domestic pets. They may have around ten dogs at a time on their premises for training. Private companies are now taking over the work of training police and military dog handlers and dogs, in searching out drugs, arms, explosives and humans. Some of these handlers are sent overseas to tackle jobs formerly dealt with by the military; training is restricted to people with a service background, and trainees are first assessed to ensure that they have a real affinity with animals.

It is worth remembering that unless you choose one of the public sector employers, only the Guide Dogs for the Blind Association has a recognised training programme. In the private sector there are no NVQs or any other structured training programmes and no state aid. The British Institute of Professional Dog Trainers call dog training a do-it-yourself profession. Ask them for their useful careers leaflet and details of their Certificates in Instructional Techniques. You could also contact the Association of Pet Dog Trainers.

Case Study

Ann is 24 and a highly skilled trainer.

'On my Easter holidays, just before I left school, I was handed a cross Labrador and told: "If you can train this dog, we'll take you on as a trainee trainer." I've never worked so hard at anything, and I did it. It's true anyone can be taught to do it, but some will never make trainers and you can tell. Equally, people who come as naturals are few and far between. You need a feeling for dogs and an understanding of them. You've got to make it clear to the dog who is in charge, but there's no point in frightening him. Take this one. She's inclined to snap, particularly when she's with her owner. She's come here to learn better manners because she had a go at a builder. Her owner thinks the dog is over-protective. Well, I think she's timid. She wants her confidence building up. She might be growling or snapping, but her ears are down and look at her tail. Right between the legs.

'We had one real delinquent here – a Yorkie that bit people. His owner wrote in despair to a very famous dog expert who wrote back advising him to take all the dog's teeth out. Well, we laughed but of course it's not really funny. We told him we thought that was a bit drastic. We use a check chain, give a sharp jerk, tell the dog off, then – when he's thought it over – a word of reassurance.

'We work the dogs here in the yard, simple commands like "sit", "heel", "down". Then we take them out. This nervous one I shall take to shopping centres, into crowds, to get her used to it. You've got to remember you're not training these dogs for yourself but for other people.

'It is a pleasure to take an untrained dog, or a badly trained one, which is worse, and work patiently with it and see it turn into an obedient, sensible animal.'

Police dogs

Police dogs attract a lot of attention. There is something fascinating about the fact that they look perfectly ordinary while everyone knows they are one. As one policeman describing an off-duty incident put it: 'I was in plain clothes at the time, and so was my dog… heavily disguised as a family pet.' Like all good disguises, that one was based on reality. Police dogs are family dogs, living with their handlers from puppyhood. Their handlers are normally married, so there is someone at home to look after the dog, and they must have a garden.

Training

The majority of dogs are gift dogs donated to the police from families who are no longer able to cope with them – dogs that in 12 months turned from cute puppies into 80lb Shepherds. If they are younger than two years they are juvenile animals that can still be trained. A Home Office qualified dog trainer learns about the dog's past and assesses its character – it must be bold but not overly aggressive, with a high play drive. Nine out of ten dogs don't fit the bill. All the other dogs are puppies allocated to a handler, who takes it home and treats it as any owner would, training it in simple obedience and building up a strong relationship with it.

All dogs go through a 12–14 week course, either at one of six regional dog training schools, or at an in-force training school. Most police dogs are trained in general-purpose police work but spaniels and labradors are taught to find drugs and explosives.

Some dogs don't qualify, which is sad for everyone, particularly the handler who has probably waited for two years to be allocated a dog. Dog and handler have to attend frequent refresher courses at one of six training centres throughout the dog's working life, which lasts about seven years. A retired dog usually remains with its handler who is then given another puppy.

A very senior policeman who spent most of his life working with dogs said: 'First you've got to want to be a copper; don't forget – there are more people who want to work with dogs than there are dogs.'

It's not possible to join the police as a handler. Two years on the beat must be completed first. Dog handlers and their dogs now have to be licensed annually.

Guide dogs

Another specialised branch of training is carried out by the Guide Dogs for the Blind Association. There are seven Client Service Centres – at Leamington, Exeter, Bolton, Forfar, Middlesbrough, Wokingham, Redbridge – and the Tollgate Breeding Centre. Each centre hires its own staff. Promotion to training assistant is usually made within the Association, so anyone hoping for this work would do well to start by finding a job as a member of the kennel staff.

Kennel staff

This is more varied than many kennels jobs. Work starts at 7 am when the kennels are cleaned before breakfast. The day is spent feeding, grooming and assisting in the education of the dogs, whilst other duties include the care of sick or post-operative dogs and some contact with future owners of the dogs. Making them welcome during their training stay at the centre, morale-boosting and practical help are part of kennel staff duties, so obviously quite a special person is looked for by the controller of a training centre.

Applicants for kennel staff must be at least 18 years old, educated to GCSE/SCE standard (or equivalent) including English language (Grades A–D). Kennel staff gain City and

Guilds Kennel Staff qualifications and can eventually take the C&G Kennel Supervisor qualification.

Salary starts at £8,992 pa and rises to £11,990 pa on qualification.

Guide dog trainers

Applicants for guide dog trainers should be at least 18 with three GCSE/SCE passes, including English language (Grades A–C). They should also have domestic or work experience with animals and work or social experience with adults. A driving licence is essential, as is an excellent physical health record and a high degree of fitness. The training leads to the City and Guilds Guide Dog Trainer qualification.

The trainers provide the dogs with the real introduction to their life's work. They take over a nine-month-old dog who has lived with a puppy walker family and ease it into its new routine.

They begin simply, taking the dog for pleasure walks, assessing it all the time. After three weeks the dog is taught to walk at a comfortable speed, how to respond to the harness it will wear as a working dog, and how to concentrate on the voice of the training assistant.

After eight weeks an obedient, responsive dog is ready to be handed over to the next trainer, a mobility instructor.

Salaries are currently not less than £11,990.

Mobility instructor

There is a three-year training course to become a mobility instructor, with an examination at the end of it. The course covers dog welfare and psychology, selection and training and aspects of veterinary care, and trainees must pass City and Guilds examinations. The trainer is also instructed in the psychology of blind people and the practice training of future owners in the use of a guide dog.

The trainer has to teach the dog how to judge height and width. It must learn that some occasions call for disobedience, such as ignoring a command to go forward into a situation it can see is dangerous. The dog is taught to regard the human at the end of its harness as an extension of itself and allow for that when it makes basic decisions, such as whether or not a space is wide enough to pass through or whether there is headroom. Naturally, this highly specialised training calls for a lot of affection from the instructor and a desire to please on the part of the dog. One of the most difficult parts of the training is helping the dog transfer its loyalty to its new owner. Mobility instructors visit the dogs in their new homes during the first few days, travelling regular routes with them and giving advice to the owners.

Salaries for qualified Guide Dog Mobility Instructors are not less than £19,540.

This is a demanding and stressful job and applicants must be at least 18 years of age. Qualifications needed are five GCSE or equivalent passes including English language, maths, a science subject and a social science subject (Grades A–C). Work experience should include dealing with groups of people from various social backgrounds, preferably including the disabled. A driving licence is essential.

Hearing Dogs for Deaf People

Although a comparatively young organisation, with fewer job opportunities than at Guide Dogs for the Blind, Hearing Dogs for Deaf People offers unique opportunities for people wanting to train dogs to understand and react to certain noises, such as a telephone, a door bell and so on.

Candidates are expected to have an outgoing personality, an interest in dog behaviour and experience in training and welfare. Membership of dog clubs, joining agility and obedience classes or training your own dog to a specialist level would all count. Registering your dog as a PAT (Pets as Therapy) dog and paying regular visits to sick and lonely people will also demonstrate interest and commitment to the concept of dogs helping people.

Previous applicants have worked in veterinary surgeries, or have worked professionally at a kennel; others are graduates with relevant degrees in zoology, psychology and animal science and some have worked for Guide Dogs for the Blind. You should have a good standard of education, with some GCSEs, and a full driving licence.

Guard dogs

Training guard dogs is a job calling for fine judgement. There is no point in turning an animal into a potential killer. It has to be taught the difference between friend and foe, how to scare off intruders, how to deal with aggression and how to defend itself and its owner's property without inflicting serious damage.

Someone has to act the part of the bad guy during training; this is not always a popular role among young trainers, whose instinct is to have a good relationship with the dogs.

Case Study

Clive *is 16 and has begun training guard dogs.*

'I do like dogs and I've always wanted to work with them, but guard dog work doesn't worry me, in fact I like it. I'd no idea if I would be good with dogs and I was a bit nervous at first. I had to start by cleaning kennels and so on, which I'm not too keen on. What I really like is training. I bait the dogs, with a stick in a sack. No, I don't think it strange for a dog lover to do that kind of thing. I enjoy making them angry. Dogs enjoy guard work. I can see why some people don't like it. The person who baits a dog has to keep out of its way after that and it really worries me that I might forget. The dog won't forget. But I'm never afraid of a dog otherwise.'

Royal Army Veterinary Corps (RAVC)

The RAVC is responsible for all animal procurement, training, management and veterinary care within the Armed Forces. About 150 soldiers work in the RAVC and although there is a limited number of positions for Farriers and Equitation specialists the main employment is with dogs. The RAVC trains dogs and handlers for guard or security duties, or for specialist tasks such as arms explosive search, drug detection or tracking. The job requires patience and concentration but is very rewarding. To enter the RAVC you'll need a minimum of four GCSEs, grades A–C, or equivalent, including English Language. Further information is available from your local Armed Forces Careers Office, listed under 'Army' in the phone book.

Pets

Pet shops

Some young people who want to work with animals make their own opportunities. Not everyone can set up their own business, although there are still surprising numbers of people who do, usually beginning by working for other people until they have the expertise.

And not everyone who begins by taking holiday jobs in a pet shop ends up managing a chain. But it can be done. Neil Fox is someone who did it at 23. He runs a pet shop near the Angel in Islington, London, and is area manager, with responsibility for several other shops.

Case Study

Jane is a pet shop manager.

'It started when I was still at school and I had a fish tank. I used to come in here to buy things for it. I just liked animals so I came around a lot, and when I left school I asked for a job.

'The day starts at 8 am, before the shop opens to the public. I let the animals out while I clean and disinfect the cages, and I let the puppies run about the shop, for exercise. Of course it's chaos, but they love it. They make a mess, but you have to tolerate that. Where else can they make a mess? Cleaning up is all part of the job.

'You do spend most of your time selling from the shelves, but every time you sell an animal you get to know the owner. They come back for food and sometimes advice, and let you know how the animal is getting on. I can tell who will give an animal a good home. They usually come in to see it once or twice before making up their minds. Then they bring the family, or the girlfriend. If I think they wouldn't look after it properly, I wouldn't sell the animal. I can just tell. Maybe I'm making a mistake, but I'd rather do that than sell an animal to a buyer who would not look after it. I just tell them it's sold.'

Fifteen thousand people work in pet shops in Britain. Duties are such that a high degree of dedication is a primary requirement. Staff working in a pet shop need to develop their knowledge of livestock husbandry, products and customer care. The only recognised qualification for pet shop employees is the City and Guilds Pet Store Management Course 776. This is available from some colleges or by correspondence through the National Extension College and the Pet Care Trust.

Animal behaviourist

Pets don't have to be naughty to be referred by a vet to a pet behaviourist. It's more likely that the owner hasn't understood what makes their animal tick. In fact, the term pet behaviourist is misleading because much of the work involves helping people. A pet behaviourist questions the owner, watches the animal's body language, analyses the problems and sets up a behaviour modification programme for the owner to follow. This may include rewarding the pet for good behaviour, changing its environment, or approaching it in a way that makes it feel at ease.

No formal qualifications are required but it is possible to study a postgraduate course – so a relevant degree or approved qualification and appropriate experience would be necessary for this. Experience of animal training and handling is essential. If you want to train on the job you will need to assist a practising behaviourist and/or attend short courses and lectures. For further information contact the Association of Pet Behaviour Counsellors and the UK Registry of Canine Behaviourists.

Animal grooming

The most usual business for those who want to set up on their own is animal grooming. As anyone who has ever forced so much as a chihuahua into a tub knows, dogs don't take joyfully to this process. And there is a great deal more to it than a canine shampoo and set.

The grooming routine includes bathing the dog, drying it (probably with a hairdrier), brushing and combing the coat, trimming the nails, cleaning teeth and ears and dealing with fleas or other parasites, if necessary. The final result is a pleasant-smelling dog with a gleaming coat.

Dog beauticians may be working for private pet owners, or for those who want to show their dogs. Although they may work for a shop – or 'parlour' – they can also work from home or within boarding or breeding kennels, a pet shop or vet's surgery.

As well as being able to handle dogs, even those that do not like being bathed, a dog beautician also has to be fit enough to spend a great deal of the day standing up. It is not a job for people with skin allergies.

Training is usually by apprenticeship with an established pet parlour or beautician, or within kennels, where the training would be included as part of general kennel work. It is important to make sure at the outset that the training will be of a good standard; it will take from one to three years. The same cautious approach should be taken with the private fee-paying courses, though most are good. These may last only three months, or a year; the longer ones should include instruction in the different styles used for the various types of dog, aspects of dog care, and practical experience.

Applicants may also secure a place on a National Traineeship programme. All training should be delivered by qualified trainers who hold the City and Guilds Dog Grooming Certificate 775, and who preferably have achieved or are working towards the Advanced Grooming Diploma. There is also a Level 2 SVQ in Dog Grooming.

All dog beauticians are advised to take these qualifications as they show potential employers and customers that you have reached a qualified level of expertise. A careers leaflet and list of approved schools is available from the British Dog Groomers Association.

Case Study

Peter *served an apprenticeship in the grooming section of a large store and has recently opened his own establishment.*

'I wouldn't say canine beautician is the best thing to tell people you do for a living, although that is the correct term. You do get some funny reactions. I get some remarks about the name of my shop too – Peter's Posh Pets. Actually, the reason for that is quite basic. I had to get the name Peter in, because previous clients knew it, and I tried to make it memorable. PPP seemed not entirely inappropriate.

'You train on the job as an apprentice – no more nerve-racking than training as a hairdresser. Less, I'd imagine. You trim a cocker spaniel a millimetre shorter on the right and he's not going to hit you with his handbag.

'I wasn't interested in training school. How do I know they're qualified to teach me? If you do this job properly, and I do, you don't just shampoo the dog and push it under the drier. You examine its teeth, clean them if necessary, make sure they're sound. You attend to their ears and nails and, when they are in the bath, express their anal glands – not pleasant, but quickly done.

'It's pretty hard work, and dirty work as well. It is usually done by girls, but I find it an advantage to have a deep voice and a forceful personality when I take on the bigger dogs. I don't have much trouble with them, but I'll muzzle a dog if it's got ideas. There's no point in being lax with them. They're like little kids. They need firm handling. I'm never afraid of a dog, although I've certainly been bitten. The minute you're afraid, the dog has won.

'This can be a seasonal job for some, although not for me because I'm uptown. Work can fall off a lot during the wet and cold season and anyone taking it up should know that. It's not well paid, frankly. I pay myself only a modest salary and there are times when all the headaches involved in running a shop make it seem hardly worthwhile.'

Animal photography

With imagination, ingenuity and a bit of lateral thinking, skills won in other areas can be put to use in animal work. At one end of the scale, an animal-mad baby-sitter of 17, suspended between school and college, suddenly realised she could make at least as much money and have at least as much fun dog-walking.

A considerably larger venture was undertaken by Sally Anne Thompson. She was determined to become a photographer, in spite of the attempts of her father, who had a studio, to put her off. He felt it was an overcrowded profession. Sally Anne persisted and created a whole new profession by combining her skill in photography with her love of animals.

Case Study

Jim is an animal photographer.

'With some photographers of animals, love of the animal comes first and photography second. I think it has to be the other way round. You must have the commercial training.

'I was lucky enough to get a job as darkroom assistant and went to night school at a polytechnic. I photographed the occasional dog, and zoo animals, then I had one of those fortunate encounters with someone who bred dogs and who encouraged me. There is a market among people who show dogs. They want photographs to send to potential buyers or use in trade publications.

'I wouldn't say you need a rapport with animals so much as some sort of idea of what a picture should look like. It's hard work too. You take a shot and people say, "That's it." They're amazed if you tell them it will take a couple of hours.

'Some dogs are nervous, and some are awkward to start with. You have to work out what makes them tick.

'Most of the show dogs, if they are worth photographing, are pretty sensible. They are used to the show ring. I photograph horses too – of course I don't take them into the studio. In fact, in almost all cases, even pet studies, I prefer to go to someone's home. It can take a day, and another day processing. Animal photographers might charge anything between £100 (or less if they were just starting out) and £1,000 per day.

'You can sell animal pictures to so many different places. I do a lot of work for books. It wouldn't cost that much today to set up, with so many good cheap cameras, but you have to be exceptional to get very far. You could go to the show jumping or eventing and send proofs to the competitors. They might be so thrilled that they will order the photographs. But it's best to start by doing it at weekends, with a guaranteed job during the week. It's also essential to get good advice on business management and accountancy. You must be prepared for competition and you really have got to have something exceptional to offer.'

Introduction

Zoos have come a long way since naturalist and explorer Sir Stamford Raffles established the Zoological Society of London in 1826. The world's first zoo, a small area of Regent's Park, housed animals with little consideration of their habitat or diet. Throughout Victoria's reign and in the early part of last century, the growing collection of animals was kept in badly constructed cages and concrete pits.

Even as late as 1968, members of the public were still able to feed the animals with left-over stale bread and sticky buns from their picnics. With 15,000 to 20,000 visitors a day in the height of summer it is easy to imagine the dietary effect.

Things are quite different now. Diet has become much more important. One of the daily duties of the keeper is to prepare a range of foodstuffs for the animals. As each species requires a slightly different diet, getting the balance right is crucial.

Habits are more considerate of animal needs, and some zoos have pioneered in-captivity breeding programmes to help re-establish a number of species in the wild.

The Federation of Zoological Gardens of Great Britain and Ireland estimates that 20 per cent of zoos are already participating in global conservation strategies for endangered species, offering some wild species the only guaranteed chance of survival. Zoos are not an alternative to habitat conservation, but they are an essential safety net for the most endangered species.

As conservation work increases, zoos will employ specialist zoologists, conservation strategists and ecologists. A degree is a prerequisite for this sort of work.

Zoologist

If you want to study animals scientifically, zoology is for you. Zoologists study anatomy, physiology, classification, distribution, behaviour and ecology. When working in zoos they usually coordinate conservation breeding programmes, collection planning and general conservation strategies. Zoologists are well qualified; 5 GCSEs (grades A–C), at least 2 A levels (biology and chemistry is the best combination) and a good BSc degree in zoology or applied zoology are all required. As competition is stiff you may also need to take a higher degree (MSc or PhD).

Apart from becoming a zoo vet (see Chapter 2) or Veterinary Nurse, the most obvious route into zoo work is to become a keeper.

Zoo keeping

Zoo keeping attracts thousands of applicants each year. The biggest employers are London Zoo and Whipsnade Wild Animal Park, but the Federation of Zoological Gardens of Great Britain and Ireland publishes a complete list of its 61 members. In addition there are another 300 wild animal collections in Britain. In total about 3,000 people have full-time positions.

Conditions of work vary and there is no set career development path or recruitment strategy. Likewise, formal educational requirements differ from place to place and it is quite possible to get work without any. Most employers insist on a probationary period before they support an individual's training programme and it is normally advantageous for applicants to have shown some commitment to animals, through either voluntary, seasonal or weekend work.

Qualifications and training

No academic qualifications are normally required, though a background of natural science at school (many zoos require five GCSEs), and an understanding of animals, are an advantage, as are relevant A levels and/or a university degree. Recruits to the keeper staff at London Zoo or Whipsnade Park are expected to have some previous experience of working with animals and a good general education. But the competition is so fierce that they usually only recruit people who have some proven ability to work with animals. This could be in a pet shop, vet surgery or another zoo. The Zoological Society's keeper staff take the City and Guilds course in Zoo Animal Management which is run by the National Extension College. This is a correspondence course supplemented by the Society with additional on-site lectures and trips to other zoos. Increasingly zoos and wildlife parts are recognising the Edexcel National Diploma in Animal Care (soon to be renamed Animal Management) and the City and Guilds National Certificate in Animal Care. There is also now a BSc in Animal Management (run by Sparsholt College in Winchester). Training arrangements, as well as salaries, vary between different zoos. Vacancies for London Zoo are usually advertised in specialist magazines, such as *Cage and Aviary Birds*. Alternatively, you can apply in writing to the Senior Personnel Officer.

What the job is really like

Contact with animals is only a small part of the day's work, which is much more taken up with cleaning out and preparing endless amounts of food. Beautiful friendships with the animals are rare. The creatures are wild and usually dangerous, the hours unsocial and the pay is not marvellous. So why do so many thousands of youngsters find this job attractive?

Senior keeper

'For a kid who really knows what he or she is taking on, who is prepared for the hard slog that each day brings, and who has no romantic ideas of a glamorous job,' said a senior keeper, 'it's a good career. But I've talked to a lot of them who think they'd like the work and most of them had a completely unrealistic picture. They've seen the camel rides or elephants' bath-time and think keepers spend their time playing games with the animals. Or else they have what a colleague of mine calls "Elsa fantasies", seeing themselves striking up a sympathetic relationship with a big cat. Believe me, the only relationship you get with a lion or a tiger is mutual respect.'

Affection for animals

An affection for animals is essential but, by itself, not enough. The same keeper said: 'There's no point in aiming for zoo work unless you have a strong feeling for animals, but that's not always what people mean when they say they like them. You need more of an interest in them than a sentimental approach.

'Now, I haven't got a dog, but if I had one, or a cat or any domestic pet, I would need a completely different attitude to it from the one I would have towards any animal in this zoo. I'd train it to behave in a manner acceptable to humans, for instance. You just can't take the same approach to wild animals, even when they appear quite tame. And you shouldn't be looking for affection from them. Respect now, that's another matter. You must have that and you have to earn it, and for me there's more reward in that.'

Routine

The day starts at 8 am and can go on as late as 7 pm. A zoo will insist on punctuality, not least because the animals do. They become accustomed to routine and looking after them is a disciplined business. It is also extremely hard work.

Scraping bird cages on a frosty morning or shovelling manure and heaving huge bundles of straw is not the side of zoo work which usually occurs to someone applying for a job. Even someone who should know can be taken aback by it. Daryl is 17, a zoo helper, and he should have had few illusions as his father works at the Zoo. But he admits: 'I'd no idea what mucking out a cage was really like.' And Daryl works with small mammals. Think of the lions' cage first thing in the morning.

It is not a job for the physically frail, male or female, for it has to be done quickly and thoroughly.

Case Study

Anne *is 27 and a qualified keeper, working in the Bird House.*

'A girl has to be prepared to work harder than the men to prove herself. I know I do. It's been a man's domain for so long. I suppose it's understandable they take a rather superior attitude to women. But a strong girl can work just as well as a strong chap. Oddly enough, although it sounds daft, I agree animals can tell the difference between the sexes. I worked in a parrot house where some of them preferred men and tried to attack me. But then they were used to men. The other thing animals recognise is authority, and if you've got that they'll respect you, male or female.

'You've got to have a real vocation for this work, but you can't be sentimental. I always wanted to work with animals. My first job was with a bird farm in Keston. I've worked in RSPCA clinics and when I was an assistant I was sent on a training scheme, helping a vet for six months. I quite enjoy this work although I wouldn't mind a spell with small animals. The funny thing is, the talking birds do actually say "Hello". I suppose it's because that's what everyone says to them.

'But really, I enjoy the job. I've been here for three years and I think things are improving. There are more chances now for girls than there were.'

Typical day

A typical day in a keeper's life moves on from cleaning to food preparation. Again, this can be physically demanding in some cases, such as in the Elephant House. Each elephant needs a hundredweight of hay every day as well as vegetables and pellet food. If an animal is refusing food a keeper has to spot that quickly and find out why. Cleaning and chopping food can occupy a surprisingly large part of a working day, particularly in the Bird House where one tray can call for more than a dozen different sorts of food. Often supervision is needed at feeding time, particularly if there is a specially dominant animal which would take more than its share.

Some creatures require hand feeding. The king penguin will not eat dead fish unless it is placed in its mouth. Some animals show off to attract a keeper's attention. For others, meal-times are exercise sessions. This is one of the reasons a keeper throws fish to sea-lions, keeping them on the go and making sure each gets a fair share.

Visitors

Keepers must always be aware of visitor activity. Before animals were completely isolated from visitors, keepers kept a record of the number of items 'lifted' from unsuspecting visitors. In one year alone, the elephants seized 14 coats, 12 handbags, 10 cameras, 8 gloves and 6 return tickets to Leicester, damaging them beyond repair.

Now the elephants are kept beyond arm's reach, the keepers have fewer irate complainers to deal with. Even so, with over a million visitors a year they must be able to look after the human species as well as they do the others. As well as taking part in public presentations on animal matters, keepers must be ready to answer questions on more general topics, always answering politely and intelligently.

Salaries

Wages vary according to age and experience and between different establishments. London Zoo offers an incremental pay scheme which rises according to experience. Trainee keepers receive £13,000 a year for three years, in which time they should complete the City and Guilds Certificate in Zoo Animal Management. On completion of the training period, they become qualified keepers and earn £16,000 a year. Qualified keepers who have at least three years' experience can apply to become senior keepers with a salary of £18,000.

Making a start

Not all members of the Federation of Zoological Gardens of Great Britain and Ireland are zoos; for example, Knowsley Safari Park, Liverpool Museum Aquarium and Vivarium, the Wildfowl and Wetlands Trust and the Dartmoor Wildlife Park.

Recruitment varies from place to place and potential employers need to be contacted individually. Enquiries should always be accompanied by a stamped addressed envelope. For advertised vacancies, look in *RATEL*, the journal of the Association of British Wild Animal Keepers (ABWAK), the weekly paper *Cage and Aviary Birds*, *International Zoo News* and local newspapers and JobCentres.

As an example London Zoo employs seasonal staff every summer. The best of these may be taken on to become keepers, but as the Zoo has thousands of applicants every year, competition is stiff. If you can't get a seasonal keeper's job, perhaps you could consider spending some time working as a general attendant, or as a volunteer. Contact your nearest zoo for details. The Federation will provide you with a list.

It is possible to work overseas, but usually only with good references and a lot of experience.

9 Agriculture

Introduction

Agriculture in Britain has come under great scrutiny in recent years. Some farming practices have had to change in the light of new discoveries, most notably BSE, and many people have started to question the sort of modern agricultural techniques that have been held responsible. Anyone becoming a farmer not only has to contend with the day-to-day farming experience, which is arduous and exhausting, but must also be capable of dealing with the myriad problems associated with modern farming, which include fluctuating prices and market conditions, livestock subsidies, European legislation and the growing concerns of the sceptical consumer. Not only this, some farmers have taken the decision to switch to organic production, with its lower yields and greater costs. As interest in organic food increases, this may well be a decision which many farmers will face in the coming years.

After the 2001 foot and mouth crisis the agriculture industry looks set to change again. The trend to larger farms, which has been evident for some years now, will accelerate as smaller farms find it difficult to compete. Employment within the industry is likely to carry on declining and the number of farmers who own their farms will also go down. New entrants to agriculture should not be put off by this. Livestock agriculture in Britain is an established industry with a viable future. Ninety-two per cent of farm businesses still employ five or fewer people and this is unlikely to change greatly in the near future. Any changes that do occur should make agriculture stronger in the long term.

The work

Some farmers have a variety of animals but most farm only one species. An agricultural worker will generally specialise and remain a herdsman or a shepherd or a pig farmer throughout their working life, and quite often beyond. As with any craft worker, it is with some regret that a farmer gives up putting to use knowledge learnt over decades.

Case Study

Iain *was an assistant shepherd in Scotland for three years, and is now seeking a job as a shepherd in Yorkshire.*

'I had a very good teacher, a shepherd who had been working with sheep for 42 years. He didn't have a very high opinion of their IQ, although he always said they weren't as stupid as they looked, and he basically liked them.

'He worked out a method, during the breeding season, of checking that all the ewes had been served by the rams and I told him he should patent it. In fact, you have to have a method of marking the ewes to make sure they will produce lambs. There's always a dominant ram and, if you don't watch, there are some rare fights. You can't allow that, of course. They can damage each other and they are valuable beasts. I've been asked whether I'm afraid of rams. The answer is, I'm careful and I have a good dog. To be truthful, I would as soon cope with a ram as a sheep in a bad temper.

'The real excitement, of course, is the lambing. You don't get that much sleep during the lambing and losing a ewe is a calamity, even to experienced shepherds. Most people know how difficult it can be then, to persuade another ewe to rear the lamb of a dead mother. There were two wee girls on the farm where I worked and every season they'd hand-rear an orphan or two. I sometimes used to think they would pray for a lamb to be bottle-fed and there were the shepherds saying their prayers that there wouldn't be any orphans.

'During the winter we take crops out to the flock, and big blocks of salt.

I remember one bad year when we had to hand-feed them. Not all the ewes are suitable for breeding, and you have to learn how to select the stock.

'It's a grand feeling when the lambing is over – if it's been a good season. But you don't put on your hat and take off for the Bahamas. They need checking all the time. There's a lot can go wrong with sheep and yes, they do roll on to their backs and get stuck. It's the weight of the fleece. You'd be surprised the people who think you just herd a flock out to the hills and leave them there.

'When I started, I thought I'd give it a year. Now I'm really hooked on the whole thing.'

Farm sizes vary enormously but however many animals you tend, the round of jobs is always the same. Take the example of a dairy herdsman.

Case Study

James works on a West Country farm with a herd of 60 cattle, small by modern standards but quite enough for him.

'There's an old song that sums it up: "I've got to milk 'em in the morning, feed 'em in the evening blues." There's a lot of job satisfaction in looking after a herd, but it certainly is demanding. It means getting up about 4 am and you can't just go back to bed if it's raining or you had a heavy night the night before. If you've ever heard cows complaining about a late invitation to the milking parlour, you'd know what I mean.

'I use a dog to help herd them in, in summer. She's a cross-bred collie and the cows respect her, but I have one which will stand up to any dog and makes a point of taking her own way in her own time. She does it to keep the respect of the herd. They have a very complex social structure, cows, and you learn to respect it.

'In winter they are indoors so it's easier in the mornings and the milking parlour can seem quite cosy on a cold rainy morning, with the radio tinkling away and the milk sloshing beautifully – that is, when nothing's gone wrong with the equipment. It's a large part of my job to make sure nothing does. Each cow has to have its udder washed before the milking cups are attached. They're all used to the routine, although I've heard some pretty hilarious stories from old hands about the introduction of milking machines.

'My wife gives me a hand usually. You've got to remove the milking cups pretty promptly when the animal has given all she intends to, so you have to keep a close watch on the jars.

'Our milk goes into a tank, and that has to be 100 per cent clean. So does the equipment, which is sterilised after each use, and the dairy has to be swabbed out each time too ... and all this before breakfast. Well, some dairymen might have time for breakfast at 4.30 but not this one, and even if I did, I'd be ready for another after milking.

'It's not all over after the morning session. I do a lot of mucky work and a lot of heavy fodder and bedding around. We rear our own calves here and I'm usually there at a calving. But it's not tiring the way a city job can be, and I know because I've done both. You don't get drained doing this work. Exhausted, yes, but a healthy exhaustion. I like the work and I like the animals. They're characters, cows.'

For those wishing to find out more, the Dairy Council produce a package called 'Looking Ahead – Careers in the Dairy Industry'. It should be available from your careers officer or direct from the National Dairy Council.

Those starting their careers will need experience first. Sometimes this comes down to visiting your local farmer, or arranging through your school a period of work experience on a farm. Maintaining contact with your local NFU secretary, agricultural markets and the local Young Farmers Club is also a good idea. If you live in a city it is still possible to get some experience on a city farm, although the majority of farm workers come from rural areas. Lantra, the agricultural training body, advise those living in urban areas to contact their nearest College of Agriculture/Horticulture and consult the *Farmers Weekly* and *Farmers Guardian* (North and Wales). Those interested in organic techniques can find useful experience through an organisation called Willing Workers On Organic Farms (WWOOF). Find out if there are any organic farms in the area.

Not only will such initial work experience help you make up your mind whether or not farming is the right career for you, it will help to prepare you for proper training.

Training

Lantra, agricultural colleges, Training and Enterprise Councils (TECs) and JobCentres can all give advice on training opportunities.

There are two basic routes to a successful career in agriculture – vocational and academic. You can follow either, whether you study full- or part-time, at college or in the workplace. However you enter agriculture you will always have the chance to study for a first degree. There are several different layers of training. Which one you begin at depends on the qualifications you already have.

Enter with GCSE grades D–G and you can start off by taking a GNVQ Foundation (Standards) qualification. After that you can take a National Traineeship (explained on page 66), a Modern Apprenticeship, a GNVQ Intermediate or Advanced qualification (Scottish Group Award), a National Diploma and Higher National Diploma, Diploma or Certificate in Higher Education, any of the four NVQ or SVQ Levels and a degree.

Although all farm jobs require some training, you may achieve the lower levels quickly. However, you should note that Lantra wants an agricultural workforce able to cope with future changes in working methods. Someone with the right qualifications is more likely to find their skills in demand. In an industry that is likely to shed 22,000 jobs in the next six years you should try to give yourself the best start, and continue to take advantage of training opportunities as they arise throughout your career.

Under their skills foresight programme Lantra have identified a need for improved farm management skills and relevant environmental and technological knowledge. A more competitive international market will increase the need for business and marketing abilities, and the rising importance of environmental issues will create a need for skills and knowledge of environmentally responsible production. In addition there are also increasing requirements for compliance with health and safety, animal welfare and produce traceability legislation. Agricultural workers who show themselves adept at training will get ahead.

Lantra provide an excellent guide to the various training opportunities called *Careers in Land-based Industries*. Anyone considering a career in agriculture should get a copy.

A list of full-time and sandwich courses available in the UK is given in the *Directory of Courses in Land Based Industries* (available only on CD ROM), £19.95 + £2.95 p&p from Farming

Press Books, Wharfedale Road, Ipswich IP1 4LG; 01473 241122. For further information about careers in farming you can write (enclosing large sae) to Lantra, or phone them on 08457 078007, charged at local rate.

National Traineeships and Modern Apprenticeships

Essential technical knowledge and practical skills can be learnt at the workplace within an organised programme of work called National Traineeship (NT) and Modern Apprenticeship (MA). NTs (which are only available in England and Wales) and MAs (available in all four UK countries) are government backed schemes aimed at young people between the ages of 16 and 24. Modern Apprentices are employed and receive a wage. Wherever possible National Trainees are employed but where they can't be they receive a training allowance. No formal entry requirements are needed for the National Traineeship but by the time you finish you will have a Level 2 NVQ/SVQ qualification as well as core skills in numeracy, communication, information technology, and other training and qualifications relevant to you and your employer. Modern Apprentices must have either 3 GCSE (grades A–D) or standard grades at credit or general (including maths and English), or have completed the National Traineeship programme. You will qualify with NVQ/SVQ Level 3 and enhanced core skills similar to the National Traineeship programme.

National Vocational Qualifications (NVQs)/Scottish Vocational Qualifications (SVQs)

Other employers will prefer to offer training without the Modern Apprenticeship framework. Trainees will still be encouraged to take one of the NVQs/SVQs available:

NVQs
Level 4 Agriculture (Livestock Management)
Level 3 Fish Husbandry
Level 2 Fish Husbandry (Fin Fish)
Level 2 Fish Husbandry (Shellfish)

Level 1 General Agriculture
Level 2 Livestock Markets (Droving Livestock)
Levels 2 and 3 Livestock Production.

SVQs

Levels 2 and 3 Fish Husbandry
Level 1 General Agriculture
Level 2 Livestock Markets (Droving Livestock)
Levels 2 and 3 Livestock Production
Levels 2 and 3 Mixed Farming
Levels 2 and 3 Poultry Production.

Pay

The basic wage for Grade 1 skilled workers in the industry as laid down by the Agricultural Wages Board is £240.86 per week (2000). Workers may receive more than this, but it relates to their responsibilities and the extra hours they work; overtime is £9.26 per hour for a Grade 1 worker. Up-to-date information on wages can be obtained from the Agricultural Wages Board. This is one of the top levels of pay, and wages differ depending on skills and age. A 16-year-old, for example, can only expect to earn about £107.00 a week.

Fish farming

According to Lantra, 7,500 people are now employed in fish farms. It is one of Britain's growing industries, with rainbow trout and Atlantic salmon, oysters, mussels and scallops being the most common crop. Although qualifications may not be essential, they are useful and further details can be obtained from Lantra.

Organic farming

Organic agriculture is one of the few agricultural success stories of the last five years. With demand outstripping supply, prices have been high, and farmers have avoided the price and income slump affecting the rest of the industry. This is perhaps one of the reasons why 10 per cent of the farming population in England and Wales have phoned the Organic Conversion Information Service since it was started in 1996. Although farmed organic land still accounts for only about 2 per cent of total farmed land in Britain the rate of increase is dramatic – in 1998 the figure was only 0.5 per cent. The growth in demand for organic produce in the UK (40 per cent per year) is faster than the growth in supply (25 per cent per year) – the difference being made up by imports. As such there are great opportunities for farmers wanting to convert.

Existing farmers can get some financial help and technical support for the conversion process but those starting from scratch would do well to look into some of the organic agriculture courses listed at the back of this book. Organic farming requires an understanding of a very different set of farming operations so the information learned in training will be very different. If you want to learn on the job you'll need to approach an organic farm directly or contact a local employment agency in the same way you would for conventional farming. The Soil Association can provide a list of farms. If you want to get some voluntary experience, contact Willing Workers on Organic Farms (WWOOF). They will introduce you to a network of reputable organic smallholdings and farms (potentially all over the world), for whom you could work for anything up to six months. Normally labour is given in return for board and lodging.

There are a number of organisations offering advice and information about organic farming but you could start off by contacting the Organic Food and Farming Centre at the Soil Association, for a list of courses and contacts (although this does cost £5).

City farms

Animals have always made good tourist attractions and many farms have opened their gates to the public to earn more money, or to provide educational resources for local school children. City farms in particular have given many children their first glimpse of pigs, chickens and horses. They provide a valuable resource for cities and although the potential for full-time employment is small, there is always work for volunteers. Contact the Federation of City Farms and Community Gardens for details.

10 Getting in and getting on

Top tips for getting into animal work

♦ Few employers are prepared to take on someone who has no experience, training or proven interest in their chosen career. By proven interest I mean tangible proof that you have worked with animals in a way that demonstrates you have an affinity with the animals you care for. This could be as straightforward as looking after pets in your spare time.

♦ Enterprise is always appreciated. Case studies in this book included the pet shop owner who turned a holiday job into a career and ended up becoming the manager of a chain of stores and the dog trainer who got a job by demonstrating to her employer that she could train a pup.

♦ If you don't already have experience, and many people interested in a career working with animals do, you should look at the options open to you. First of all you will need to make a choice. Out of all the careers mentioned in this book which one are you most suited to, considering your personality, skills and attributes? Deciding what sort of animal work you want means finding out quite a bit about yourself.

♦ If you haven't already considered volunteering, do so. Not only is this a good way of finding out more about yourself, it often provides the first contact with a potential employer and gives you an opportunity to learn about the job you are hoping to do.

◆ Potential employers will be impressed by individuals who give up their time for free, particularly if you have had to suffer some material hardship, putting off the chance to earn money for example. In some cases, this is the only way of making an impression.

◆ Some people may ask you to prove yourself by working for them for nothing first. Take care not to be exploited. Any commitment on your part should be for short periods only – a week or two at the most. Some organisations run legitimate schemes which may last up to six months. The RSPB and London Zoo are good examples of these, where a period of voluntary work is the only way to make your abilities known to the employer.

◆ Not all jobs are like this, though, and you should always check out the specific demands of each career. The best people to talk to are the organisations listed in this book. Find out from them what is expected of you. They will usually have an appropriate information sheet/pack and may be able to spend some time talking to you.

◆ They may also be able to give you valuable contacts. As in all employment sectors, contacts are as important as qualifications, experience and ability. Many jobs aren't advertised and those who are lucky have often made their own luck, finding themselves 'in the right place at the right time'. Sometimes a chance letter to a potential employer can do more good than a dozen applications.

The future of animal work

A career working with animals will continue to be a popular choice among school leavers. In substance the work is unlikely to change dramatically. Animals will always require care and attention. More likely to change are the techniques with which we offer this care and attention.

Veterinary surgeons will continue to update the type of treatment they offer sick animals, whether this be through conventionally applied medicine or in the new field of animal homeopathy (the treatment of an animal as a whole rather than the treatment of a specific complaint). The profession maintains a balanced entry from year to year and this is unlikely to change in the foreseeable future. The same can be said for veterinary nurses, whose employment is directly related to the number of vets.

The number of animal welfare organisations has increased as a response on the one hand to a greater level of consciousness regarding the humane treatment of animals, and on the other hand a seemingly continuous rise in the number of reported cases of animal abuse. Incongruously, at the same time we seem to care more and less about our animals.

Animal conservation has become a topic of much debate, as the human desire for material wealth continues to conflict with the survival of animals in the wild: not just in Britain where wildlife is threatened by a sustained building and roads programme, but abroad in areas where the policies of developing countries threaten endangered species still further. Even so, if you compare this sector with some of the others in this book, such as agriculture, opportunities are much rarer and harder to come by. The sector lacks the training structures associated with some of the other sectors and entry quite often happens in a much more unpredictable way.

A total of 54,300 people are employed in equine activities and that figure is predicted to rise by 9,000 in the next six years – although this forecast by Lantra does not include the effect of any possible ban on hunting. Of the total workforce, 63 per cent are estimated to be self-employed, and with higher insurance costs, Uniform Business Rates and the cost of complying with health and safety regulations and EU regulations, this option is becoming more complicated; often people lack the necessary managerial, administrative and business planning skills. The industry has reported a growing interest in animal welfare and the environment, and many colleges – faced by demands from prospective students – have developed new animal care courses and invested considerable sums of money on indoor riding areas and equine physiotherapy pools. Overall the industry is expected to remain buoyant.

The number and size of zoos continue to shrink, as rising costs combine with lower visitor figures, and tighter animal care and welfare standards. Those that continue to operate may well recruit veterinary nurses as a regular part of zoo staff. Zoos are beginning to re-evaluate their role as they attempt to establish themselves as a key player in the battle to conserve endangered species through in-captivity breeding programmes. An estimated 20 per cent of all zoos are currently engaged in what the Federation of Zoological Gardens describe as serious research to breed species in captivity. Over the next four to five years international cooperation will increase, especially with the use of the Internet for communication and animal exchange.

The pet trade continues to expand; check out the new range of services offered by some entrepreneurs, including pet astrology and pet funerals and the new pet supermarkets. The Pet Care Trust, which acts as an industry watchdog and training provider, does not predict any significant changes in the next two or three years.

Agriculture is changing faster than any other occupation in

this book – and not without reason. International competition, BSE, foot and mouth and global climate change are all challenging accepted agricultural practice and no one can really say what will result. Some trends are obvious. The trend to larger farms will make it harder for smaller farms to compete – forcing them to close or market their product more successfully. As a result of this and other changes, the industry is likely to shed 22,000 jobs in the next six years. The news is not all bad though. The industry training organisation Lantra have identified a need for greater technical and management skills and knowledge of environmentally sensitive farming practices – including organic agriculture.

Organic agriculture is one of the few farming success stories of the last five years. The growth in demand for organic produce in the UK (40 per cent per year) is faster than the growth in supply (25 per cent per year) – the difference being made up by imports. As such there are great opportunities for farmers wanting to convert or start their careers in organic farming. Ten per cent of the farming population in England and Wales have already phoned the Organic Conversion Information Service since it started in 1996 and the total acreage of farm land in Britain under organic production has risen from 0.5 per cent in 1998 to 2 per cent in 2001.

12 Qualifications available

Many jobs require at least some level of general academic qualification before applicants can start to undertake vocational
training. Although it is still possible to get work without them,
the accepted entry point standard is four GCSE passes at C
grade or above, two of which should be maths and English.

This is not always the case and this book has already listed
examples of courses which allow you to reach the equivalent
academic standard. Pre-vocational courses enable those who do
not meet the GCSE standard, but nevertheless show a vocation
for the job, to start vocational training that will lead to full-time
employment. For example, veterinary nurses can take a pre-
vocational qualification at 16 and vocational training at 17,
without losing any time over GCSE students.

Vocational training usually starts at 16 and A-level qualifications aren't required for most jobs. One of the few exceptions
to this is the vet, who will have very good A-level results before
beginning the long degree course. Some areas of animal
research also demand high academic standards and agricultural
students can take a vocational route through university.

For most people, training begins on the job between the ages
of 16 and 18. Most of the training is free and in some regions
students are given credits to buy the training they want. These
credit schemes vary depending on where you live, so contact
your local careers office who will have full details of schemes in
your area. There are a number of different training options to
choose from.

National Vocational Qualifications (NVQs) and Scottish Vocational Qualifications (SVQs) are post-16 industry training standards for school leavers. They are assessed in a work situation, either at a college or in a job. Students take study units, some based on practical skills and others based on written work, with a range of requirements.

Different units can be built up in a complete NVQ/SVQ. Most colleges offer NVQ/SVQ courses, and the qualifications are designed to give employers an idea of a job candidate's capabilities, both in the UK and, eventually, throughout Europe. There are four levels of qualification – one to four – and each individual sector will have its own expected standards.

The following NVQs are available in England and Wales: Level 4 Agriculture (Livestock Management); Level 1 Animal Care; Level 3 Animal Training; Level 3 Animal Welfare and Management; Level 2 Caring for Animals; Level 3 Farriery; Level 3 Fish Husbandry; Level 2 Fish Husbandry (Fin Fish); Level 2 Fish Husbandry (Shellfish); Levels 2 and 3 Gamekeeping; Level 1 General Agriculture; Levels 1 and 2 Horse Care; Level 3 Horse Management; Level 2 Livestock Markets (Droving Livestock); Levels 2 and 3 Livestock Production; Levels 2 and 3 Mixed Farming; Level 3 Pet Care and Supply; Levels 2 and 3 Poultry Production; Level 2 Racehorse Care; Level 3 Racehorse Care and Management; Level 2 and 3 Veterinary Nursing.

The following SVQs are available in Scotland: Level 1 Animal Care; Level 3 Animal Training; Level 3 Animal Welfare and Management; Level 2 Caring for Animals; Level 2 Dog Grooming; Levels 2 and 3 Fish Husbandry; Levels 2, 3 and 4 Fishing Vessel Engineering; Levels 2, 3 and 4 Fishing Vessel Operation; Levels 2 and 3 Gamekeeping; Level 1 General Agriculture; Levels 1 and 2 Horse Care; Level 3 Horse Care and Management; Level 2 Livestock Markets (Droving Livestock); Levels 2 and 3 Livestock Production; Levels 2 and 3 Mixed Farming; Levels 2 and 3 Poultry Production; Levels 2 and 3 Veterinary Nursing.

General National Vocational Qualifications are designed to offer students a broadly based qualification which is something of a cross between academic and vocational training programmes. The courses are normally full time and offered at three levels: Foundation, Intermediate and Advanced. Whereas the NVQ will prepare you for a specific job, the GNVQ allows you to keep your options open, preparing you instead for a range of jobs. The GNVQ Land and Environment is a modular course with a number of relevant modules relating to caring for animals. Contact the GNVQ helpline for details: 020 7509 5556.

Neither of these has replaced the BTEC Certificate and Diploma or Scottish Certificate and Diploma courses, which offer a similar training pattern, as students advance from National Certificate to the Higher National Diploma and degree. Agricultural students often choose this route as it combines college taught management skills with practical farm experience. Most agricultural colleges have their own farms so it is still possible to get good 'hands-on' experience. For a full list of course units available, students should refer to the publications produced by BTEC and the Scottish Qualification Authority.

National Certificate (NC) courses last for one year and anyone over 17, with at least one year's practical farming experience, is eligible. Holders of the NC, or those with four GCSE passes (grades A-C), are then eligible to gain entry to a National Diploma (ND) course. These are organised on a two-year full-time or three-year sandwich basis, with the middle year spent working. The next stage up, the BTEC Higher National Diploma, is science-based, designed as it is for students who wish to work in posts demanding managerial and technological skills. You must be aged 18 or over and have either one A-level in a science subject, a BTEC National award or a level 3 NVQ or GNVQ. The course lasts two years full time or three years sandwich.

Essential technical knowledge and practical skills can be learnt at the workplace within an organised programme of work called National Traineeship (NT) and Modern Apprenticeship (MA). NTs (which are only available in England and Wales) and MAs (available in all four UK countries) are government-backed schemes aimed at young people between the ages of 16 and 24. Modern Apprentices are employed and receive a wage. Wherever possible, National Trainees are employed but where they can't be they receive a training allowance. No formal entry requirements are needed for the National Traineeship but by the time you finish you will have a Level 2 NVQ/SVQ qualification as well as core skills in numeracy, communication, information technology and other training and qualifications relevant to you and your employer. Modern Apprenticeships must have either 3 GCSE grade D or Standard Grades at credit or general (including maths and English) or have completed the National Traineeship programme. You will qualify with NVQ/SVQ Level 3 and enhanced core skills similar to the National Traineeship programme.

The horse industry has taken the lead and offers Modern Apprenticeships through the National Horse Education and Training Company, from which a number of useful leaflets are available. Modern Apprenticeships and National Traineeships are usually organised on a local basis and your local Training and Enterprise Council (TEC) or Local Enterprise Company (LEC) in Scotland should already be setting up schemes in your area. If there isn't already an established contact for animal work, encourage them to look for one by showing that you are enthusiastic. Enthusiasm always impresses people. You might even be able to persuade a local employer yourself that you are a suitable candidate.

If you do not have the necessary skills to go straight into a job with training or if you are unsure about the career you want, you could consider Skill Build. Skill Build supports 16- and 17-year-olds who have problems with basic skills such as literacy and numeracy and prepares them for the other options already mentioned.

13 Where to study

Section one: degree courses in veterinary science

Bristol
Veterinary Admissions Clerk, University of Bristol, Senate House, Bristol BS8 1TH; 0117 928 7679; www.bristol.ac.uk

Cambridge
The Department Secretary, Department of Clinical Veterinary Medicine, University of Cambridge, Madingley Road, Cambridge CB3 0ES; 01223 337600; www.cam.ac.uk

Edinburgh
The Dean, Faculty of Veterinary Medicine, Royal (Dick) School of Veterinary Studies, University of Edinburgh, Summerhall, Edinburgh EH9 1QH; 0131 650 6178; www.ed.ac.uk

Glasgow
Admissions Officer, University of Glasgow, Veterinary School, 464 Bearsden Road, Bearsden, Glasgow G61 1QH; 0141 330 5705; www.gla.ac.uk

Liverpool
The Admissions Tutor, Faculty of Veterinary Science, University of Liverpool, Liverpool L69 3BX; 0151 794 4281; www.liv.ac.uk

London

The Head of Registry, The Royal Veterinary College, Royal College Street, London, NW1 0TU; 020 7468 5000; www.rvc.ac.uk

Section two: college courses

A number of colleges offer courses in Veterinary Nursing, Animal Care, Animal Behaviour, Animal Welfare, Animal Science, Dog Grooming, Pet Care and Management, Equine Studies and Agriculture. The following is a list of these colleges. Each college is listed under county names so you can easily find out which one is closest to you. After the college name is a list of acronyms. These indicate the type of courses available. The following key is used:

Agriculture – **Ag**	Dog Grooming – **DG**
Animal Behaviour – **AB**	Equine Studies – **Eq**
Animal Care – **AC**	Pet Care and Management – **PCM**
Animal Science – **AS**	Stud Work – **Eq(s)**
Animal Welfare – **AW**	Veterinary Nursing – **VN**

The name Equine Studies is a catch-all and colleges will provide exact details of courses on offer, but they may include the British Horse Society examinations, BTEC and SCOTVEC Certificates and Diplomas, NVQs and SVQs, GNVQs and a number of other related qualifications. Unfortunately, space does not permit a complete course listing.

The following list cannot claim to be conclusive. Courses change each year so check the institute's Web site or prospectus for full details. The list does not include universities teaching zoology. For this information get a copy of the UCAS handbook or visit their Web site www.ucas.com. You should also check out www.careersworld.net. From here you can link to the Web site of any British university. Another good site is www.coursefinder.org.uk. If you want to check out what postgraduate courses are available in Britain, visit www.prospects.csu.man.ac. It should also be noted that subjects such as animal behaviour, dog grooming and animal welfare are often taught as components of animal care courses.

England: college listing by county

Berkshire
Berkshire College of Agriculture   **VN, AC, Eq, Ag**
Hall Place, Burchetts Green, Maidenhead SL6 6QR; 01628 824444; www.berks-coll-ag.ac.uk

Bristol
University of Bristol School of Veterinary Science   **VN**
Langford BS18 7DU; 0117 928 9517; www.bristol.ac.uk

Cambridgeshire
College of West Anglia   **VN, AC, Eq(s), Ag**
Landbeach Road, Milton, Cambridge CB4 6DB; 01223 860701; www.col-westanglia.ac.uk

College of Animal Welfare   **VN, AC**
Wood Green Animal Shelters, Godmanchester, Huntingdon PE18 8LJ; 01480 831177

Cheshire
Reaseheath College   **AB, AC, AW, Eq, Ag**
Reaseheath, Nantwich CW5 6DF; 01270 625131; www.reaseheath.ac.uk

Cornwall
Duchy College of Agriculture   **VN, AC, Eq, Ag**
Stoke Climsland, Callington PL17 8PB; 01209 722100; www.cornwall/duchy.ac.uk

Cumbria
Cumbria Campus, University of Central Lancashire   **AC, AS, Eq, Ag**
Newton Rigg, Penrith CA11 0AH; 01768 863791; www.uclan.ac.uk

Derbyshire
Broomfield College   **AC, Ag**
Morley, Ilkeston, Derby DE7 6DN; 01332 831345;
www.broomfield.ac.uk

Devon
Bicton College of Agriculture   **VN, AC, DG, PCM, Eq, Ag**
East Budleigh, Budleigh Salterton EX9 7BY; 01395 568353;
www.bicton.ac.uk

Dorset
Bournemouth & Poole College of Further Education   **VN, AC, DG, Eq**
North Road, Parkstone, Poole BH14 0LS; 01202 747600;
www.thecollege.co.uk

Kingston Maurward College   **VN, AC, Eq, Ag**
Dorchester DT2 8PY; 01305 215000; www.kmc.ac.uk

Lynwood College of Veterinary Nursing   **VN**
Station Road, Wimborne, Dorset BH21 1RQ; 01202 882101

Durham
East Durham and Houghall Community College   **VN, AC, DG, Eq, Ag**
Houghall, Durham DH1 3SG; 0191 386 1351;
www.edhcc.ac.uk

Essex
Writtle College   **VN, AC, DG, Eq, Ag**
Writtle, Chelmsford CM1 3RR; 01245 420705;
www.writtle.ac.uk

Gloucestershire
Abbeydale Veterinary Training   **VN**
20 Glevum Way, Abbeydale GL4 9BL; 01452 300596

Hartpury College   **VN, AC, AS, AB, AW, Eq, Ag**
Hartpury House, Hartpury GL19 3BE; 01452 700283;
www.hartpury.ac.uk

Royal Agricultural College   **Eq, Ag**
Cirencester GL7 6JS; 01285 652531

Hampshire
Farnborough College of Technology   **VN, Eq**
Boundary Road, Farnborough GU14 6SB; 01252 405555;
www.farn-ct.ac.uk

Sparsholt College   **VN, AC, Eq, Ag**
Sparsholt, Winchester SO21 2NF; 01962 797280/776441;
www.sparsholt.ac.uk

Hereford
Holme Lacy College   **VN, AC, AW, PCM, Eq, Ag**
Holme Lacy HR2 6LL; 01432 870316; www.pershore.ac.uk

Hertfordshire
Oaklands College   **VN, AC, Eq, Ag**
Oakland Campus, Hatfield Road, St Albans AL4 0JA; 01727
737000; www.oaklands.ac.uk

Kent
Hadlow College of Agriculture and Horticulture   **VN, AC,
PCM, Eq, Ag**
Hadlow, Tonbridge TN11 0AL; 01732 850551;
www.hadlow.ac.uk

Springboard Bromley   **DG, AC, Eq**
Bromley College, Rookery Lane, Bromley BR2 8HE; 020
8462 1222

Thanet College   **Eq**
Ramsgate Road, Broadstairs CT10 1PN; 01843 605040

Lancashire
Myerscough Collge   **VN, AC, Eq, Ag**
Myerscough Hall, Bilsbarrow, Preston PR3 0RY; 01995
640611; www.myerscough.ac.uk

Leicestershire
Brooksby College   **AC, Eq, Ag**
Brooksby, Melton Mowbray LE14 2LJ; 01664 850850;
www.brooksbymelton.ac.uk

Lincolnshire
De Montford University Lincoln   **AC, AB, AW, Eq, Ag**
School of Agriculture & Horticulture, Caythorpe Court,
Caythorpe, Grantham NG32 3EP; 01400 275572;
www.dmu.ac.uk

London
Kingsway   **VN**
c/o Cerberus Training and Consultancy, Yewgate Cottage,
Remensham Hills, Henley-on-Thames RG9 3ES; 01491
414113; www.kingsway.ac.uk

Manchester
North Trafford College of Further Education   **VN, AC, DG**
Talbot Road, Stretford, Manchester M32 0XH; 0161 872
3731; www.northtrafford.ac.uk

Merseyside
City of Liverpool Community College   **Ag**
Old Swan, Broad Green Road, Liverpool L13 5SQ; 0151 252
3000; www.liv-coll.ac.uk

Middlesex
Capel Manor   **AC, Eq, Ag and saddlery** (formerly taught at
Cordwainers College)
Horticultural and Environmental Centre, Bullsmoor Lane,
Enfield EN1 4RQ; 020 8366 4442

Norfolk
Easton College   **AC, Eq, Ag**
Equestrian Centre, Easton, Norwich NR9 5DX; 01603
731200

Northamptonshire
Moulton College of Agriculture and Horticulture   **VN, AC,
DG, Eq, Ag**
West Street, Moulton, Northampton NN3 7RR; 01604
491131; www.moulton.ac.uk

Nottinghamshire
Brackenhurst College   **AC, AS, Eq, Ag**
Brackenhurst, Southwell NG25 0QF; 01636 817000;
www.ntu.ac.uk

Oxfordshire
Abingdon and Witney College   **AC, Eq(s), AG**
Holloway Road, Witney OX3 7EE; 01993 703464

Shropshire
Harper Adams University College   **AC, AS, AW, Eq, Eq (saddlery), Ag**
Newport, Shropshire TF10 8NB; 01952 815000; www.harper-adams.ac.uk

Walford and North Shropshire College   **AC, Eq, Ag**
Baschurch, Shrewsbury SY4 2HL; 01939 262100; www.wnsc.ac.uk

Somerset
Cannington College   **AC, AS, Eq, Ag**
Cannington, Bridgewater TA5 2LS; 01278 655000; www.cannington.ac.uk

Staffordshire
Rodbaston College of Agriculture   **VN, AC, AS, Eq, Ag**
Penkridge, Stafford ST19 5PH; 01785 712209; www.rodbaston.ac.uk

Suffolk
Otley College   **VN, AC, AS, DG, Eq, Ag**
Otley, Ipswich IP6 9EY; 01473 785543; www.otleycollege.ac.uk

Surrey
Merrist Wood   **AC, Eq**
Worplesdon, Guildford GU3 3PE; 01483 884000; www.merristwood.ac.uk

NESCOT (North East Surrey College of Technology)   **AC, AS**
Reigate Road, Ewell LT17 3DS; 020 8394 1731; www.nescot.ac.uk

Sussex
Brinsbury College of Agriculture and Horticulture   **AC, VN, Eq, Ag**
North Heath, Pulborough, West Sussex RH20 1DL; 01798 877400; www.brinsbury.ac.uk

Plumpton College **AC, Eq, Ag**
Plumpton, Lewes, East Sussex BN7 3AE; 01273 890454;
www.plumpton.ac.uk

Warwickshire
Warwickshire College of Agriculture **VN, AC, Eq, Ag**
Moreton Hall, Moreton Morrell CV35 9BL; 01926 318333;
www.warkscol.ac.uk

Wiltshire
Lackham Wiltshire College **VN, AC, AS, Eq, Ag**
Lacock, Nr Chippenham SN15 2NY; 01249 466800;
www.lackham.ac.uk

Worcestershire
Worcestershire College of Agriculture **AC, VN, Eq(s), Ag**
Hindlip, Worcester WR3 8SS; 01905 451310;
www.pershore.ac.uk

Yorkshire
Askham Bryan College **AC, Eq, Ag**
Askham Bryan, York YO2 3PR; 01904 772277; www.askham-bryan.ac.uk

Bishop Burton College of Agriculture **AC, Eq, Ag**
York Road, Bishop Burton, Beverley, East Yorkshire HU17
8QG; 01964 553000; www.bishop-college.ac.uk

Queen Ethelburga's College (School) Equestrian Centre **Eq**
Thorpe Underwood Hall, Ouseburn, York YO26 9SS; 0870
7423300

Rotherham College of Arts and Technology **VN**
Eastwood Lane, Rotherham S65 1EG; 01709 362111;
www.rotherham.ac.uk

Scotland

Borders College **AC, Eq, Ag**
Melrose Road, Galashiels TD1 2AF; 01896 757755;
www.borderscollege.ac.uk

Clinterty Agricultural College **Eq, Ag**
Kinellar, Aberdeen AB5 0TZ; 01224 612751

Edinburgh's Telford College **VN**
Crewe Toll, Edinburgh EH4 2NZ; 0131 332 2491; www.ed-col.ac.uk

The North Highland College **VN, Eq**
Ormlie Road, Thurso, Caithness KW14 7EE; 01847 896161;
www.nhi.ac.uk

Oatridge Agricultural College **AC, Eq, Ag**
Ecclesmacham, Broxburn, West Lothian EH2 6NH; 01506
854387; www.oatridge.ac.uk

Scottish Agricultural College **AS, Ag**
581 King Street, Aberdeen AB24 5UD; 01224 711000
Auchincruive, Ayr KA6 5HW; 01292 520331
West Mains Road, Edinburgh EH9 3JG; 0131 667 1041;
www.sac.ac.uk

University of Glasgow **VN**
Veterinary School, 464 Bearsden Road, Bearsden, Glasgow
G61 1QH; 0141 330 5700; www.gla.ac.uk

Wales

Coleg Sir Gar **AC, AS, PCM, Eq, Ag**
Land-Based Industries Division, Pibwrlwyd, Carmarthenshire
SA31 2NH; 01554 748000; www.ccta.ac.uk

Coleg Meirion Dwyfor Glynllifon **AC, Eq, Ag**
Fford Clynnog, Caernarfon, Gwynedd LL54 5DU; 01286
830261; www.meirion-dwyfor.ac.uk

Coleg Powys **Ag**
Agricultural Department, Llanidloes Road, Newtown, Powys
SY16 1BE; 01686 622722: www.coleg-powys.ac.uk

Gwent Tertiary College **AC, PCM, Eq**
Usk Campus, The Rhadyr, Usk, Gwent NP5 1XJ; 01495
333639; www.coleggwent.ac.uk

Pembrokeshire College **AC, Eq, Ag**
Haverfordwest, Pembrokeshire SA61 1SZ; 01437 765247;
www.pembrokeshire.ac.uk

Pencoed College   **AC, Eq, AG**
Pencoed, Bridgend, Mid Glamorgan CF35 5LG; 01656 302600

The University of Wales, Aberystwyth/Welsh Institute of Rural Studies   **AS, Eq, Ag**
Llanbadarn Fawr, Aberystwyth, Dyfed SY23 3AL; 01970 622021; www.wirs.aber.ac.uk

Yale College   **Eq**
Grove Park Road, Wrexham, Clwyd LL12 7AA; 01978 311794; www.yale-wrexham.ac.uk

Northern Ireland

Enniskillen College of Agriculture   **Eq, Ag**
Levaghy, Enniskillen, County Fermanagh BT74 4GF; 028 6634 8000; www.enniskillencollege.ac.uk

Greenmount College of Agriculture and Horticulture   **Ag**
22 Greenmount Road, Antrim BT41 4PU; 028 9442 6666

The Queen's University of Belfast, Faculty of Agriculture and Food Science   **AS, Ag**
Newforge Lane, Belfast BT9 5PX; 028 9025 5202; www.qub.ac.uk

Section three: correspondence courses

Animal Care College
29a Ascot House, High Street, Ascot, Berkshire SL5 7JG; 01344 628269

The Animal Care College is recognised by the Council for the Accreditation of Correspondence Colleges. Students pay a registration fee of £20, which also gives them membership of the Institute of Animal Care Education. No formal qualifications are required before an application can be made except in the case of veterinary nursing, but some courses require candidates to be employed in the industry before they begin. Courses are Complementary Therapies for Pets, Introduction to Small

Animal Care, Certificate in Pet Dog Ownership, Fit for Life –
Training the Family Dog, Introduction to Canine Psychology,
Intermediate Canine Psychology, Intermediate Feline Psych-
ology, Intermediate Animal Behaviour, General Certificate of
Canine Studies, Diploma in Companion Animal Bereavement
Counselling, Grooming Theory, National Small Animal Care
Certificate – Level 2, Advanced Canine Psychology, Advanced
Animal Behaviour, Canine Behaviour – Counselling Theory
and Practice, Behavioural Modification for Professionals,
The Instructor's Certificate, Advanced Instructor's Certificate,
Judging Diploma, The Dog Breeding Diploma, Veterinary
Nursing Correspondence Course, Diploma of Kennel
Management, Diploma in Advanced Canine and/or Feline
Care and several Advanced Short Courses.

National Extension College
Michael Young Centre, Purbeck Road, Cambridge CB2 2HN;
01223 316644; www.nec.ac.uk
In conjunction with the National Federation of Zoological
Gardens, offers City and Guilds Animal Management (7630).

Pet Care Trust
Bedford Business Centre, 170 Mile Road, Bedford MK42 9UP;
01234 273933
Offers City and Guilds Pet Store Management (7760).

14 Useful addresses

All the following can provide information and advice about a career working with animals. Please send a stamped and self-addressed envelope for replies.

Agricultural Wages Board, Nobel House, 17 Smith Square, London SW1P 3JR; 0845 0000134

Animal Care College, Ascot House, High Street, Ascot, Berkshire SL5 7JG; 01344 628269; www.animalcarecollege.co.uk

Animal Health Trust, PO Box 5, Shailwell Road, Newmarket, Suffolk CB8 7DW; 01638 661111

The Animal Welfare Trust, Tyler's Way, Watford Bypass, Watford, Hertfordshire WD25 8WT; 020 8950 8215

Association of British Riding Schools, Queens Chambers, 38–40 Queen Street, Penzance, Cornwall TR18 4BH; 01736 369440

Association of British Wild Animal Keepers, 4 Llys Close, Oswestry, Shropshire SY11 2UZ; www.abwak.co.uk

Association of Pet Dog Trainers, Peacocks Farm, Northchapel, Petworth, West Sussex GU28 9JB; 01428 707234; www.apdt.co.uk

Association of Pet Behaviour Counsellors, PO Box 46, Worcester WR8 9YS; 01386 751151; www.apbc.org.uk

Battersea Dogs Home, 4 Battersea Park Road, London
SW8 4AA; 020 7622 3626

Bell Mead Training College for Kennel Staff, Priest Hill
House, Priest Hill, Old Windsor, Berkshire SL4 2JN; 01784
431599

The Blue Cross, Shilton Road, Burford, Oxfordshire OX18
4PF; 01993 822651; www.bluecross.org.uk

Association of British Dogs and Cats Homes, Battersea
Dogs Home, Battersea Park Road, London SW8 4AA; 020
7622 3626; www.dogshome.org

**British Association of Homeopathic Veterinary
Surgeons**, Alternative Veterinary Medicine Centre, Chinham
House, Stanford-in-the-Vale, Faringdon, Oxon, SN7 8QN;
01367 718115

British Dog Groomers Association, Bedford Business
Centre, 170 Mile Road, Bedford MK42 9TW; 01234 273933;
www.petcare.org.uk

The British Horse Society, Stoneleigh, Warwickshire CV8
2LR; 08701 202244; www.bhs.org.uk

British Institute of Professional Dog Trainers, Bowstone
Gate, Nr Disley, Cheshire SK12 2AW; 01663 762772;
www.bipdt.net

British Racing School, Snailwell Road, Newmarket, Suffolk
CB8 7NU; 01638 665103; www.brs.org.uk

British Trust for Conservation Volunteers, 36 St Mary's
Street, Wallingford, Oxon OX10 0EU; 01491 839766;
www.btcv.org.uk

British Veterinary Nursing Association (BVNA), Level
15, Terminus House, Terminus Street, Harlow, Essex CM20
1XA; www.bvna.org.uk

**Department for Environment, Food and Rural Affairs
(DEFRA)**, State Veterinary Service, 1a Page Street, London
SW1P 4PQ; 020 7904 6000

The Donkey Sanctuary, Sidmouth, Devon EX10 0NU; 01395 578222; www.thedonkeysanctuary.org.uk

Earthwatch Europe, 57 Woodstock Road, Oxford OX2 6HJ; 01865 318838; www.earthwatch.org

Edexcel, Customer Enquiries Unit, Stewart House, 32 Russell Square, London WC1B 5DN; 08702 409800; www.edexcel.org.uk

Farriers Registration Council and Farriery Training Service, Sefton House, Adam Court, Newark Road, Peterborough PE1 5PP; 01733 319770

Federation of Zoological Gardens of Great Britain and Ireland, London Zoo, Zoological Gardens, Regent's Park, London NW1 4RY; 020 7586 0230

The Guide Dogs for the Blind Association, Hillfields, Burghfield, Reading, Berkshire RG7 3YG; 0118 983 5555; www.gdba.org.uk

Hand to Paw, 9 Skimmington Cottages, Bonnys Road, Reigate, Surrey RH2 8RL; 01737 242873

Hearing Dogs for Deaf People, The Training Centre, London Road (A40), Lewknor, Oxfordshire OX49 5RY; 01844 353898

International Animal Rescue, Animal Tracks, Ash Mill, South Molton, Devon EX36 4QW; 01435 831185

International League for the Protection of Horses, Anne Colvin House, Snetterton, Norwich NR16 2LR; 01953 498682; www.ilph.org

International Zoo News Subscription Department, 80 Cleveland Road, Chichester, West Sussex PO19 2HF; 01243 782803; www.zoonews.ws

The Kennel Club, 1 Clarges Street, Piccadilly, London W1Y 8AB; 0870 6066750; www.the-kennel-club.org.uk

Lantra, Lantra House, NAC, Kenilworth, Warwickshire CV8 2LG; 0845 707 8007; www.lantra.co.uk

Monkey Sanctuary, Nr Looe, Cornwall PL13 1NZ; 01503
262532; www.monkeysanctuary.org

**National Association of Farriers, Blacksmiths and
Agricultural Engineers,** The Forge, Avenue B, Tenth Street,
NAC, Stoneleigh, Warwickshire CV8 2LG; 01203 696595

National Canine Defence League, 17 Wakley Street,
London EC1V 7RQ; 020 7837 0006; www.ncdl.org.uk

National Dairy Council, 5–7 John Prince's Street, London
W1M 0AP; 020 7499 7822; www.milk.co.uk

National Dog Wardens Association, 5 Talgarth Road,
Ashley Down, Bristol BS7 9LN

National Extension College, Michael Young Centre,
Purbeck Road, Cambridge CB2 2HN; 01223 450200;
www.nec.ac.uk

Federation of City Farms and Community Gardens,
The Green House, Hereford Street, Bedminster, Bristol BS3
4NA; 0117 923 1800; www.farmgarden.org.uk

National Greyhound Racing Club Ltd, Twyman House,
16 Bonny Street, London NW1 9QD; 020 7267 9256

National Pony Society, Willingdon House, 102 High Street,
Alton, Hampshire GU34 1EN; 01420 88333;
www.nationalponysociety.org.uk

National Stud, Newmarket, Suffolk CB8 0XE; 01638
663464; www.nationalstud.co.uk

Northern Racing College, The Stables, Rossington Hall,
Great North Road, Doncaster DN11 0HN; 01302 861000;
www.northernracingcollege.co.uk

Organic Food and Farming Centre, Soil Association,
Bristol House, 40–56 Victoria Street BS1 6BY; 0117 929 0661;
www.soilassociation.org

PDSA, PR Department, Whitechapel Way, Priorslee, Telford,
Shropshire TF2 9PQ; 01952 290999; www.pdsa.org.uk

Pet Care Trust, Bedford Business Centre, 170 Mile Road, Bedford MK42 9TW; 01234 273933

Pets As Therapy, National Head Office, Rocky Bank, 4–6 New Road, Ditton, Aylesford, Kent ME20 6AD; 01732 872222; www.pat-prodog.org.uk

Qualifications and Curriculum Authority, 83 Piccadilly, London W1J 8QA; 020 7509 5555; www.qca.org.uk

The British Horseracing Training Board (BHTB), Suite 16, Unit 8, Kings Court, Willie Snaith Road, Newmarket, Suffolk CB8 9BL; 01638 560743

Recruitment and Assessment Services, Alencon Link, Basingstoke, Hampshire RG21 3JB; 01256 329222 – For applications to MAFF posts only; they do not send out careers information

Royal Army Veterinary Corps, Defence Animal Centre, Melton Mowbray, Leicestershire LE13 0SL; 01664 411811

Royal College of Veterinary Surgeons, Belgravia House, 62–64 Horseferry Road, London SW1P 2AF; 020 7202 0736; www.rcvs.org.uk

Royal Society for the Protection of Birds (RSPB), The Lodge, Sandy, Bedfordshire SG19 2DL; 01767 680551; www.rspb.org.uk

RSPCA, Wilberforce Way, Southwater, Horsham, West Sussex RH13 7WN; 0870 0101181; www.rspca.org.uk

Scottish Qualifications Authority, Hanover House, 24 Douglas Street, Glasgow G2 1NQ; 0141 242 2214; www.sqa.org.uk

Scottish Society for the Prevention of Cruelty to Animals, Braehead Mains, 603 Queensferry Road, Edinburgh EH4 6EA; 0131 339 0222

Scottish Wildlife Trust, Cramond House, Cramond, Glebe Road, Edinburgh EH4 6NS; 0131 312 7765; www.swt.org.uk

Society of Homeopaths, 4a Artizan Road, Northampton NN1 4HU; 01604 621400

Society of Master Saddlers, Kettles Farm, Mickfield, Stowmarket, Suffolk IP14 6BY; 01449 711642

Stable Lads Association, 74 High Street, Swadlincote, Derbyshire; 01283 211522

Thoroughbred Breeders' Association, Stanstead House, The Avenue, Newmarket, Suffolk CB8 9AA; 01638 661321; www.tbassoc.demon.co.uk

UK Registry of Canine Behaviourists, Patricia White, Secretary UKRCB, 53A Oxford Gardens, London W10 5UJ; 020 8969 5670; www.ukrcb.co.uk

Universities and Colleges Admissions Service (UCAS), PO Box 40, Cheltenham, Gloucester GL50 3SB; 01242 227788; www.ucas.com

Universities Federation for Animal Welfare, The Old School, Brewhouse Hill, Wheathampstead, Herts AL4 8AN; 01582 831818; www.ufaw.org.uk

The Veterinary Record, 7 Mansfield Street, London W1G 9NQ; 020 7636 6541; www.vetrecord.co.uk

Whipsnade Wild Animal Park, Dunstable, Bedfordshire LU6 2LF; 01582 872171; www.whipsnade.co.uk

Wildfowl and Wetlands Trust, Slimbridge Centre, Gloucestershire GL2 7BT; 01453 890333; www.wwt.org.uk

Willing Workers on Organic Farms (WWOOF), Main Office, PO Box 2675, Lewes, East Sussex BN7 1RB; 01273 476286

Wood Green College of Animal Welfare/Animal Care Industry Lead Body, Wood Green Animal Shelters, Godmanchester, Huntingdon, Cambridgeshire PE18 8LJ; 01480 831177

Northern Ireland

Conservation Volunteers Northern Ireland, 159 Raven Hill Road, Belfast BT6 0BP; 028 9064 5169; www.cvni.org

Department of Agriculture, Dundonald House, Upper Newtownards Road, Belfast BT4 3SB

Guide Dogs for the Blind, Lanesborough House, 15 Sandown Park South, Belfast BT5 6HE; 028 9047 1453; www.gdba.org.uk

Republic of Ireland

Blue Cross Dublin Clinic, 8 Orwell Road, Rathgar, Dublin 6; 00 353 1497 1709; www.bluecross.ie

Conservation Volunteers Ireland, 65a Harold Cross Road, Dublic 6W; 00 353 1454 7185; www.cvi.ie

Irish Guide Dogs for the Blind, Model Farm Road, Cork 00 353 2148 70929; www.guidedogs.ie

Irish National Stud Company Ltd, Tully, Kildare, County Kildare; 00 353 45 521251; www.irish-national-stud.ie

Irish RSPCA, 300 Lower Rathmines Road, Dublin 6; 00 353 1497 7874; www.rspca.ie

The Veterinary Council of Ireland, 53 Lansdowne Road, Ballsbridge, Dublin 4; 00 353 1668 4402; www.vci.ie

15 Further reading

Vets

Training to be a Veterinary Surgeon (free)

Veterinary nursing

A recommended reading list and a number of free careers leaflets are available from the British Veterinary Nursing Association on receipt of an sae.

Animal welfare and conservation charities

Animal Contacts Directory (£4.95) Veggies
Directory of Environmental Courses (available in careers libraries)
    The Environment Council
*Green Volunteers, The World Guide to Voluntary Work in Nature
    Conservation* (£10.99) Vacation Work; 01865 241978

Working with horses

British Equestrian Directory (£11.95) EMC & BETA; 01937
    582111
A Career in the Horse Industry (£9.95) Kenilworth Press,
    Addington, Buckingham MK18 2JR; 01296 715101
Careers in the Horseracing Industry (free) British Horseracing
    Training Board

Racing Post and *Horse and Hound* – journals available from most newsagents

Where to Ride (£5.95) British Horse Society

Working with dogs

Dog Training Weekly, incorporating *Obedience Competitor*, supply a recommended reading list for potential dog trainers. Their address is Prince House, Parc Y Shwt, Fishguard, Pembrokeshire SA65 9AP; 01348 875011. Alternatively, your local library may be able to order one of the following; *Training the Family Dog* by John Holmes; *Living with Dogs* by George Summers; *Understanding Your Dog* by Peter Griffiths; and *Heel Away Your Dog* by Charles Wilde.

How to Work with Dogs (£9.99), The Pet Behaviour Centre, Upper Street, Defford, Worcestershire WR8 9AB 01386 750615

Working with Dogs and Other Animals (free) National Canine Defence League

Pets

The Pet Care Trust will send out free leaflets on working in a pet shop and dog grooming.

Zoos

The Federation of Zoological Gardens of Great Britain and Ireland will send you a number of leaflets regarding conservation, education, welfare and careers. The Universities Federation for Animal Welfare produce videos on caring for animals.

Agriculture

Careers in Land-based Industries (free) Lantra.

Directory of Courses in Land Based Industries (£19.95), Farming Press Books, 01473 241122 (CD ROM only)

Index

Lightning Source UK Ltd.
Milton Keynes UK
16 August 2010

158491UK00001B/183/A